STYLE

STYLE

John Haynes

London and New York

First published 1995
by Routledge
11 New Fetter Lane, London EC4P 4EE

Transferred to Digital Printing 2003

Simultaneously published in the USA and Canada
by Routledge
29 West 35th Street, New York, NY 10001

Typeset in Times Ten and Univers by Florencetype Ltd,
Stoodleigh, Devon

British Library Cataloguing in Publication Data
A catalogue record for this book is available from the British Library

Library of Congress Cataloguing in Publication Data
A catalogue record for this book has been requested

ISBN 0-415–10396–7

CONTENTS

ACKNOWLEDGEMENTS

Acknowledgements are due to the following: BBC Radio Sport for permission to quote from the commentary on the Boxing contest between Bruno and Coetzer; Secker and Warburg for permission to quote Miroslav Holub's poem, 'Brief thoughts on the letter M'; Faber for permission to quote from e.e. cummings' poem 'anyone lived in a pretty how town'. The extract from *Pinocchio* by Carlo Collodi on p. 74 has been reproduced with permission of the Estate of the Late Dr E. Harden. Thanks are due also to Richard Hudson for comments and advice on earlier drafts of this book.

INTRODUCTION

This is an introduction for the nonspecialist to the kind of things which nowadays are studied under the heading of 'style'. No attempt has been made to define style, or to adjudicate among the very many different conceptions of it, or its relations to the central concerns of linguistics, to psychology, social theory or literature. Definitions can come later. The priority here is to give the reader a taste of what writers on style do, and of the different tactics they may adopt.

But since this is an introduction the emphasis is placed on foundations, that is, on helping the reader to develop an interest in and sensitivity to words and structures. These, after all, can be studied in a relatively objective way; and if the beginner does not have some competence at this nuts-and-bolts level there is every danger that the subjective element – which plays a valid part, willy-nilly, in every discussion of style – will run out of control. Studying style may be very much more than a fascination with words, but is nothing much without it.

Some readers may come to this book with the expectation that 'style' means 'literary style', as indeed it has tended to in the past. There is one unit devoted specifically to poetic aspects of style, but the viewpoint from which the book is written is that literary texts are to be studied in the same general way as are other kinds of text.

The book is set out in a number of units, each devoted to a particular aspect of style, and in the appendix there is a collection of the texts used to illustrate different types of analysis. You will need to refer to these texts as you work your way through the book.

It is perhaps worth pointing out that the word 'text' is used, in what follows, not only of written language, but of spoken also. So a telephone conversation, a lecture, a conversation over the garden fence are texts just as much as novels, recipes or love letters.

A note on the activities set out at the end of each unit. The idea of these is to allow the reader, ideally in discussion with others, to reflect on the ideas put forward in the unit, and, in particular, to have a go at using some of the concepts and methods illustrated. They are focused on the process of analysis, on encouraging the reader to take responsibility for his or her findings, hunches, viewpoints and puzzlements. So no canonical 'answers' are provided.

CHOOSING *LE MOT JUSTE*

1

> A very common view of style is that it is a matter of the careful choice of exactly the right word or phrase, *le mot juste*.

The simplest way of looking at this is in terms of SYNONYMS. In a fairy tale, do we say *ass* or *donkey*? In the office, do we say *shorthand typist* or *stenographer*? At the optician's do we say *glasses* or *spectacles*? At Christmas do we say *present* or *gift*? At the meeting, *chairman*, *chairperson* or *chair*?

In actual speaking or writing synonyms are not such straightforward entities as may appear from a dictionary of synonyms and antonyms. This is because although two words may be very similar in meaning there are almost always differences of nuance, differences of impact on a listener or reader. Saying *spectacles* is not quite the same as saying *glasses*. Saying *chairman* has a different impact from saying *chair*.

Since so-called synonyms are never quite equivalent we cannot simply say that style is 'same meaning different words'. What we might say is that words such as *glasses* and *spectacles* overlap a good deal in their meaning, and that the study of style is the study of finer shades of meaning within a more general commonness.

These 'finer shades' may be of different types. For example, two words referring to the same thing may do so from different points of view, as when the same person is referred to as a *terrorist* by enemies, and as a *freedom fighter* by friends. Sometimes the difference between synonyms will be related to the kind of text in which they occur, as when a horse is termed *grey* by those who habitually live and work with horses, but *white* by an outsider. Synonyms may differ from the point of view of politeness, as when someone says *excrement* to avoid a four-letter word. They may differ from the point of view

3

of formality, as when we say *rodent operative* rather than *rat catcher*. Or they may differ in assertiveness or emphasis, as when someone answers *right* when they might have said *yes*. Or synonyms may differ from the point of view of economy of space as with *UK* as against *United Kingdom*. This example also illustrates that there may be more than one reason for opting for a particular synonymn. Thus *UK* not only takes up less space to write, it is also slightly less formal.

Choosing the right word is also a matter of how we focus on what we are talking or writing about. For example the same motor vehicle may be referred to as a *car* or a *Toyota*. *Toyota* is more specific, a closer focus, as it were, and also more economical since it includes the meaning 'car'. It is a matter of focus, again, when we choose to refer to something by mentioning just a part of it, as when the gangster demands *wheels*, meaning a whole car. This again is an economy provided the listener follows the meaning.

Tenor

Other options, such as saying *old banger* for *car*, or metaphors such as *pig* for a person we dislike, bring in personal evaluation, or make a gesture of informality to the reader or listener, and are connected to the TENOR of what we are saying or writing, that is, the personal and power relations involved.

Let us look at an imaginary situation. You want to sell your car. You decide to write a small advertisement for your evening paper. Naturally this requires a number of decisions about wording. Let us concentrate on just one. You want to make a sentence in which you mention your car and then say 'for sale'. How will you fill in the blank in '—— for sale'. On the back of an envelope you try out some wordings. In these, you are referring to the same thing, your car, but you are not expressing exactly the same meaning. Looked at in this way, style is a matter of presentation. Consider:

(a) car
(b) motorcar
(c) automobile
(d) family saloon
(e) Fiesta
(f) banger
(g) wheels

These overlap in meaning in different ways. The first three are very close, but differ (in the British context) in the effect they generally produce. *Car* is the most casual everyday term, *motorcar* is slightly more formal and dignified, *automobile* more so, and perhaps a shade archaic in Britain.

Examples (d) – (g) still cover the general meaning 'car' but refer to types of car. Example (f), *banger*, is also informal, and jokey, and (g) perhaps suggests a 'gangster' jargon.

The choice of items for inclusion in an advertisement depends on how you want to represent the car and in doing so how 'economical with the truth' you want to be, and it also depends on your judgement as to who the likely buyer might be and what approach might appeal to such a buyer. What do you say?

(h) Car for sale.
(i) Dream car going for a song.
(j) Do you want a lovely car?
(k) Buy this car before someone else snaps it up!
(l) Car. One owner. 17k miles. As new.

These all have the same purpose, to persuade a reader to come and look at the car. But they 'come on' in different ways. (h) is a neutral announcement. (i) is informal and colloquial but still announcing. (j) moves from announcement to a question and the somewhat emotive 'lovely'. (k) gives a kind of command to the reader, and a warning. (l) lists important selling points.

There are a large number of ways in which something can be represented. It will be useful, however, to bear in mind two general categories when thinking about the choice of words. These are:

(a) choices of words to do with what is selected for focus of attention (*Toyota* rather than *car* or *vehicle*);
(b) choices that establish a relationship with the reader or listener (*banger* rather than *car* or *automobile*).

✐ **EXERCISES**

1.1 Assess the following pairs of words from the point of view of their stylistic differences. Concentrate on differences in focus. For example:

Is a detail used to suggest a whole? Or vice-versa? Example: *hand* for *worker*.

Is the difference one of evaluation or ideological point of view? Example: *terrorist* for *freedom fighter*.

Is the difference to do with formality/informality? Example: *residence* for *home*.

Is the difference one of emotional involvement/detachment? Example: *home* for *house*.

Is it a matter of 'in' jargon/everyday wording? Example: *tabs* for *curtains* (in a theatre).

Naturally some of the examples will differ in more than one way, and you should point that out. For example 'tabs' is both an 'in' term for stage curtains, and is also more informal.

(a) dinner, dindins
(b) a bite, a meal
(c) traveller, hippy
(d) His Excellency the Life President, that stomach-full-of-bilge
(e) f.y.i.a., for your immediate attention

(f) Pat, Patricia
(g) for the fuller figure, for fat women
(h) Get your arse over here, Please could you come here
(i) white horse, grey
(j) very palatable, yummy

1.2 A cafe owner wants to attract children to her cafe. She has devised an ice-cream dish with cream, chocolate sauce, strawberries and dessicated coconut in it. Invent three different two- or three-word phrases for

(a) the title for the cafe (specially catering for ice cream, for children);
(b) the name of the ice cream (on the menu, containing cream, chocolate sauce, strawberries and dessicated coconut).

You may invent new words, provided their meaning is clear, and/or you may use unconventional spellings. The three examples you devise should differ as to:

(i) focus of attention (e.g. on taste, size, ingredients, stylishness);
(ii) relation to the reader (e.g. degree of assumed familiarity, decorum, flattery as to status).

The same example can be looked at from the viewpoints of (i) and (ii). For example *Whoppa* focuses attention on size (i), and assumes a familiar slangy relation to the reader (ii).

1.3 Rewrite the following made-up headlines so as to make them less formal and more 'tabloid'. You may use fewer letters and spaces between words than the examples given, but not more.

(a) TEENAGERS BURN CAR
(b) YOUNG CHILD ABDUCTED
(c) VAT POLICY REVIEW

1.4 Imagine these are the opening sentences of short stories. The author uses the technique of mentioning significant parts or aspects of things and leaves the reader to work out the whole. Give glosses on what is left unsaid. Suggest a person and place.

(a) High heels came clicking down the corridor.
(b) I change to fifth and put my foot down.
(c) When the green light flashed, she put the green bit of wood with 8 on it on the hook and went in.

1.5 Here are some pairs of words which are very close in meaning and which have a different 'feel'; but this is very difficult to account for and you may feel that anything you say is subjective. Discuss the examples and try to make your responses explicit. Make a note of any example where you began feeling that the difference was subjective but conversation made things feel less so.

   (a) football, soccer
   (b) sweater, jumper
   (c) sofa, settee
   (d) signal, sign
   (e) rubbish, refuse

2 FOLLOWING AND FLOUTING CONVENTIONS

> Whenever we actually speak or write we are affected by social and linguistic conventions and by the expectations of readers or hearers.

All kinds of speaking and writing have conventional rules. Answering the phone, it is conventional to say 'hello' and to say who you are. In writing an essay it is conventional to put your name at the top, and the title, and to follow accepted rules of argument, coherence, paragraphing in standard polite English. And so on. These are conventions we habitually follow, though we may not be consciously aware of them. But they impress themselves on us, nevertheless, when they are broken. Thus when we open a letter from the bank manager and read

(1) Dear Mr Brown

the fact that letter-writing conventions are being followed does not necessarily strike us, for the very reason that they are, in fact, being followed. Example (1) is what we expect. The oddness of the bank manager's addressing us as 'dear' is neutralised by its usualness. But should we receive a note from the bank manager which began

(2) You undisciplined bloody spendthrift!

our sense of convention would be aroused quite sharply. This would be because the conventions have been broken and we feel the absence of the innocuous normal 'Dear Mr Brown'.

Style may be based on following conventions, as in (1), or on flouting them, as in (2).

Example (1) is not mere ritual, however, because within the genre of the business letter from the bank manager there are conventional options. He might write (1) or

(3) Dear Sir

or even

(4) Dear Fred Brown

These are all based on the convention that you begin a letter with something like 'Dear Fred'. Let us call this the 'greeting'. But what you actually write can vary greatly while still carrying the basic purpose of greeting and getting the letter started.

Your exact wording will depend on who you are writing to, in what capacity. If you are writing to someone for the first time and the context is formal and the person is a man you normally begin

(5) Dear Sir

After a few letters have gone between you, you move on to

(6) Dear Mr Brown

and then, with closer acquaintance

(7) Dear Fred

and after longer friendship you may use Fred's schoolboy nickname from way back

(8) Dear Piggy

There are variations on this. If the context of your letter has to do with Brown's position as a Royal Air Force officer, you may, instead of (6), write

(9) Dear Squadron Leader Brown

or, in place of (5), if you are writing a formal official letter as a person from the ranks, you would begin

(10) Sir

If there is a wide gap between you and Brown in age or status, but the relationship is warm, you may begin

(11) My dear Brown

which sounds a little old-fashioned now, or

(12) My dear Fred

If your relationship is one of lover or spouse you might begin

(13) Darling Fred

or, slightly stronger,

(14) My darling

or even the now rather old-fashioned

(15) Dearest Fred

or

(16) Dearest

If you have been married some time your greetings might be that much more staid, for example:

(17) My dear

These are conventional matters on the whole, and the example of letter writing is a useful example because the conventions here are fairly clear. However, once a friendship or love affair has developed beyond a certain point the conventions themselves may begin to be relaxed, or used ironically, or humorously. Now, instead of making use of the socially laid down conventions, we may start to tinker with them.

(18) Hi Fred!

replaces the conventional 'Dear ...' opening by a more conversational kind of greeting. But the purpose it serves is the same as the conventional kind of greeting.

A lover might begin

(19) Scrumptious!

substituting a kind of *ad hoc* nickname for a greeting.

If Brown were now an elderly Battle of Britain veteran, an old comrade might begin with a 'greeting' designed to recall old times:

(20) Achtung!

or

(21) Red Leader!

Here the writer is beginning to flout the conventions by re-inventing letter greetings him- or herself. The communication by letter is being played out as communication by fighter pilot's intercom. One kind of greeting is used metaphorically to serve as another.

But the conventions can be used ironically. For example

(22) Darling Squadron Leader

at first sounds contradictory because the formal is mixed with the intimate. But in a particular context, let us say, where the writer is in fact the squadron leader's fiancée and is writing to congratulate Fred on his promotion, the kicking over the traces of convention makes sense. The writer is expressing affection by making a point of using the new title.

Similarly, the kind of greeting which would be appropriate in a newspaper agony column,

(23) Dear henpecked of Sittingbourne

could be used as a joking greeting by the newly wed bride.

Another factor is politeness. Sometimes a more formal than necessary greeting will be used to show annoyance or rudeness. So

> **(24) Dear Mr Brown**

could be used to indicate that the friendship on the writer's side had cooled. Again, an upstart nephew might cause offence by writing in an over-familiar way, and using the Squadron Leader's schoolboy nickname,

> **(25) Dear Piggy**

The letter greetings have been looked at because they are clearcut examples. In them it so happens that the conventions (and their flouting) are primarily to do with the relations between the writer and the reader. However, this is not the only way in which conventions provide a basis upon which expectations are set up.

Jokes, for example, often depend on the listener's expectations, often not about status, but about the relations between words and context. All kinds of writing or speaking have conventions, in the sense of an expected 'normal' style, though this is not always easy to state in a clearcut way. The general point can be seen intuitively, however, if we imagine someone writing the minutes of a meeting in the language of a boxing commentary, or making a marriage proposal following the conventions of a television interview, or in the example of the 1960s group who sang the Highway Code as if it were a psalm.

✐ **EXERCISES**

2.1 Order the following letter 'goodbyes' in a list with the most formal at the top and the most familiar at the bottom. Items which you think are of equal status can be listed together.

(a) Yours
(b) Yours truly
(c) Yours respectfully
(d) Sincerely
(e) Chow!
(f) Love from
(g) Luv
(h) Yours faithfully
(i) Your affectionate niece
(j) Your obedient servant
(k) With all my love

2.2 Jokes often hinge upon someone leading an audience to expect one thing but supplying something different, yet fitting, in an unexpected way. Comment on the following, noting what the expected answer would be in each case. The comedian's punchlines are based on an unconventional interpretation of key words. Explain the unconventional interpretation in each joke.

(a) COMEDIAN   You know what my father always calls me?
STRAIGHT MAN   No. What?
COMEDIAN   He always calls me Johnny.
STRAIGHT MAN   Why's that?
COMEDIAN   It's my name.

(b) STRAIGHT MAN   Would you call me a taxi, please.
COMEDIAN   Okay. You're a taxi.

(c) STRAIGHT MAN   Who was that lady I saw you with last night.
COMEDIAN   That was no lady. That was my wife.

2.3 The following examples lead the reader to expect something conventional and then disappoint the expectation. Note down the kind of continuation which would be expected, but does not occur.

(a) Join the army. Travel the world. Meet all sorts of exotic interesting people. And kill them.
(b) Do me a favour, will you? Drop dead!
(c) Most people put manure on their strawberries. I prefer cream.

2.4 Spelling can be used for stylistic effect, and often is in commercial advertising. Explain how the following spellings (i) are unconventional and (ii) do still conform to spelling rules of a kind. For example, the spelling *Beatles* is unconventional in not being *Beetles*, but conventional in the looser sense that *-eat* can be used in English to represent the appropriate sound.

(a) Beanz meanz Heinz.
(b) Drinka pinta milka day.
(c) Spud-U-like.

2.5 Explain how the following set up expectations which they then flout.

(a) Go to work on an egg.
(b) Get a head. (sign on hairdresser's)
(c) Her daily male.

LIVE AND DEAD METAPHORS

3

This unit deals with metaphor, which is understood as the way in which words may be used in texts and contexts where they are not familiar or expected, though with usage they may become, as it were, naturalised to these new homes.

Metaphors, however striking, have a way of being repeated and so of growing less unexpected, and then after a time of being almost unnoticeable. We then call them 'dead' metaphors. This is a misleading way of putting things, however, to which we will return. But first, let us consider the so-called 'LIVE' or original METAPHOR.

'Live' Metaphor

Someone is watching a much-admired rock singer performing on stage. They write in a letter afterwards:

(1) She sang in a halo of spotlight.

The word *halo* does occur, in a specialist sense, in scientific texts, but it is more commonly associated with religion. Saints and prophets have haloes over or behind their heads. The metaphor, then, has the effect of connecting saintliness and heavenly glory to the world of rock music. Through the metaphor the rock star is presented as someone to be venerated. Both *halo* and *spotlight* are types of light in circular shape, on (or behind) the face. These are features of meaning the words have in common both in the context of religious paintings and in the rock concert. The difference is that *halo* is 'at home' in the context of holiness and veneration, while spotlight is not, or at least not especially connected with it. The way the metaphor works is for the suggestion of 'veneration' to be transferred over into the context of rock music, and for other characteristics of each sphere to be left out of consideration. The metaphor is produced to compare the sense of adoration saint and rock star may evoke, but we are not supposed to carry over other features of the saintly life such as modesty, poverty and celibacy.

Table 3.1 sets this out. The items put in square brackets are related but contrasted words which might be expected in one or other of the contexts.

Table 3.1 *Halo* as a metaphor

	Halo	*Spotlight*
Meanings in common	light circular around head	light circular around head
Meaning transferred from *halo* context to *spotlight* context	venerated ⟶	
Aspects of the contexts which have to be suppressed	[religious [humble [poor [celibate	commercial] exhibitionist] commercial] erotic]

In looking at metaphor, then, we are looking at two things: first the way in which one social context is brought into contact with another (rock/saintliness); and second the way in which this involves transferring selected components of meaning from the word in its familiar context, and suppressing others.

The striking kind of metaphor we have just talked about is not the only kind. A distinction is commonly made between 'live' and 'dead' metaphors. *Halo* as discussed would count as *live*. A so-called 'DEAD' METAPHOR is one which has been taken on as a normal way of saying things so that we now think of it as literal. It evolves with the language. An example would be the word *bulb* applied in the context of electric lighting. At an earlier point in our history, when there was no electricity, *bulb* was used exclusively in a horticultural sense, to do with onions and tulips and so on. The basis of its use for an electric light is the shape. But now we think of the term *bulb* or *light bulb* without thinking of plants or making a comparison between the contexts. A similar evolution occurred more recently in the Hausa language, when electricity was introduced. The Hausas use the word *kwai* for *light bulb*; but it does not mean 'bulbous root', it means 'egg'. Here the comparison is based not only on the shape of eggs and light bulbs, but also on the common qualities of brittleness and having a shell with something more vital inside.

The distinction between 'live' and 'dead' metaphors can be misleading, because it suggests that 'dead' metaphors are spent forces. In fact the 'dead' metaphors are often very much alive. The very fact that we may not recognise them as metaphors can affect our thinking without our realising it. Politicians and people in advertising have often made use of this.

Among so-called 'dead' metaphors some are very much more influential than others, depending on the role they play in social and

'Dead' metaphor

cultural life. Here is a well-discussed example. We often say that some-one has something 'in' his or her mind. This does not sound like a metaphor at first, for the reason just mentioned, that we have grown so used to it. But it is metaphorical in that it is based on an unstated assumption that the mind is a kind of container which thoughts, ideas, memories, calculations can be placed or take place 'in'. This metaphor, although 'dead', is far from inactive. Every time we use it we unconsciously channel our thoughts in a particular direction. The philosopher Gilbert Ryle, in his seminal book *The Concept of Mind* has drawn attention to the lasting influence of this metaphor. And later writers in politically orientated stylistics have emphasised the way in which this way of talking about the mind, and so of thinking about the mind, is linked to a western ideology of individualism, with the idea that a person is 'in his own head', self-contained and self-consistent.

Because the container metaphor is familiar we fail to see anything problematical, or indeed ideological, about it. And because it seems to reflect everyday common sense we may not realise that we are not talking about the mind as such but about a particular way of viewing the mind. We may go on to draw conclusions which depend more on the metaphor than what we really know about minds. If the mind is a container then education may be thought of as a method of 'filling' it, or 'storing' it with 'contents' and a 'stock' of knowledge. And although there may be a lot to be said for such a view, there will be some people who regard it with suspicion. It tends to encourage a view of human minds as passive, education as collecting 'contents' to be 'stored', and hence it may promote a particular ideology. All this in turn may well affect how we think about education as such, and knowledge, and thinking.

Instead of talking about 'live' or 'dead' metaphors it might be better to think in terms of 'original' and 'conventional' metaphors.

✐ **EXERCISES**

3.1 Here are some conventional (so-called 'dead') metaphors.

What context is the metaphorical word drawn from?
What is the basis of the comparison?
What contradictions between the contexts are suppressed?

You may want to look some of these up in an etymological diction-ary, or make your own speculations.

(a) singing star
(b) delivering the curriculum
(c) salt cellar
(d) mole (kind of spy)

3.2 Here are some common conventional metaphors which make use of aspects of the weather to describe some aspect of human character or feelings. A famous example of this sort of metaphor is Shakespeare's phrase 'the winter of our discontent'.

Rewrite each one so as to make it original, but use the same general kind of comparison between the weather and an aspect of human character or experience. For example, the metaphor *an icy smile* could be rewritten as *an arctic smile*, or *a fridge–freezer of a smile*, or *a polar grin*. *Mental fog* could be redescribed as *mental air pollution, cerebral exhaust fumes*.

(a) a stormy character
(b) waves of emotion
(c) a sunny disposition
(d) a hail of invective
(e) a whirlwind romance

3.3 Sometimes metaphors are based on other than single words or short phrases. An example is where a question is used as a command, for example 'Would you like to open the window' spoken by a general to a private. This is not a request for information about what the private would like to do!

Consider the following questions and statements and think of contexts in which they would have a different force from the most obvious or 'literal' one of asking for information or something to be done, or giving information.

(a) I'm hungry!
(b) Is that an ice-cream parlour?
(c) Do you have ten pence?
(d) You will not do that ever again.
(e) Does that give you pleasure?

3.4 Imagine three kinds of text, a boxing commentary, a political speech and a story about Pinocchio. From the list of words and phrases below pick out

(a) Words which, when not used as original ('live') metaphors, fit into one type of text only. An example would be *knock-out*, which is 'at home' in boxing or wrestling texts.
(b) Words which fit into more than one type of text. An example would be *win* which might fit into a political text (winning an election) or in a boxing text (winning a bout). Indicate the differences in meaning for each text type.
(c) Words from (a) and (b) which could be used metaphorically in a different text type, or types. Indicate the meaning of the metaphor. An example would be *knock-out* which could be used in politics to describe a successful speech.

Words and phrases

punch, on the ropes, Britain, economy, puppet, carved, left, eyes, nose, heavyweight, governing

---

3.5 Many proverbs are metaphors. An apparently straightforward comment or question or command is made with the understanding that it will be understood metaphorically. Thus, 'Rabbits go into their burrows when it rains' could be interpreted metaphorically to mean, 'It is sensible to take precautions to protect yourself when things are bad'. What happens is that we first interpret the comment about rabbits as a generalisation. This is not itself metaphorical. But then, we apply it to a particular situation, perhaps to do with our particular job security during the recession.

Suggest proverbial meanings for the following.

(a) Lions only roar when they are hungry.
(b) Empty the rubbish bin when it's full.
(c) You've got to eat your greens!
(d) Fasten your seat-belt before take-off.
(e) The cake's already been cut.

4   PATTERNS OF WORDS IN A TEXT

> Style is also a matter of the verbal patterning of a text as a whole, and the stylistic unity to which this patterning gives rise.

So far we have discussed style in relation to single words and short phrases. But we have to remember that the style of a text is not made by the writer or speaker's making a succession of (usually spontaneous) separate choices. One choice affects another, and the overall stylistical 'feel' of a text derives from the pattern which all these specific choices make. Also, the kind of text being made exerts an overall influence over individual verbal choices. The boxing commentator is constrained by the genre to speak in a particular way, and to use particular kinds of words and sentences.

The idea of an overall pattern can be illustrated by looking at the following list of words which come from the boxing commentary.

List 4.1

cover up	jab	cross
break	corner	ring
bell	left-hand	dance
target	low	clinch

These words also have other 'homes'. A 'cross' in boxing is not the same as a 'cross' in soccer; a heavyweight's 'dancing' is not a ballerina's; a boxer's target is not an archer's, or a business executive's. But they all nevertheless fit together as typical boxing commentary words. And also, we naturally interpet the words in ways which fit into boxing rather than, for example, soccer or business meetings.

We thus have a set of words, let us say, in a television commentary on a boxing contest, in which some words and phrases will be particularly associated with boxing, but which also occur elsewhere still carrying their boxing connotations – *clinch* for example; some words will be associated with boxing but also with other contexts, but when used in the boxing commentary take on specifically boxing meanings – for example *target*. Other words will be more readily associated with other contexts – *dancing* – but take on a metaphorically adjusted meaning in the boxing text. Other words still, the very common ones such as *and*, *in*, *it*, will not be particularly affected by the boxing text, but may be used as part of a different kind of pattern. An example (a negative one) is the tendency *not* to use *is* and *he* where they might be expected in other kinds of text.

The boxing commentator unconsciously takes all these matters into account in choosing his words, and a typical 'boxing commentary' texture emerges.

This can best be appreciated if we look at a stretch of actual commentary. Text A(i) covers the first minute of the first round of the contest between Frank Bruno and Coetzer in a radio commentary. You will find it in the appendix.

The context of professional heavyweight boxing is shown in four broad ways, as far as the choice of individual words and phrases is concerned. These are set out in List 4.2. The words and phrases under (a) are to do with the people concerned. List (b) contains 'boxing words', though many of them are ordinary enough, such as *punch*, *holding*, *fight*, *right*, but they take on relatively specialist meanings. Punching, to be legal in boxing, has to be done in a particular way. The 'fight' is not a free-for-all. *Right* means a punch delivered with the right (gloved) fist. And so on. Of course there is not an absolutely clearcut line between these words and those listed under (c), words about the human body.

> *List 4.2*
>
> (a) *Boxing people*
>> Words and phrases referring to participants whom the informed listener will immediately associate with boxing:
>>
>> **Coetzer (6), Bruno (6), Riddick Bowe (the champion), Alan Taweel (coach), Roy Francis (referee).**
>
> (b) *Boxing words (in this context)*
>> Words and phrases associated with boxing, but not exclusively so, but here taking on a technical status:
>>
>> **throw/throwing (3), overhead right, ramrod left jab, fight, backed up, corner, ropes, holds/holding on (2), leather, coach, left over the top, scoring punch, land clubbing rights.**

(c) *Body words*

Words and phrases for aspects of the body which are pertinent to boxing, such as the fighters' weights.

taller, six foot four, clings, head (2), back.

(d) *attack/defend words*

General words and phrases to do with attacking and defending:

come out (2), aggressive intent, thudded into, attack, on to the offensive.

These are, of course, target and source of all the action in the text. More general attacking and defending words and phrases occur (d). The latter, however, do not require specialist interpretation. *Attack* is not a technical term in boxing in the way *hold* and *right* are. But obviously in listening to a boxing commentary we imagine *attack* in a particular boxing way.

The student of style is interested in patterning of this kind, that is, the way in which the choice of words is effected in a consistent way over a passage or text as a whole. Often such patterns can be brought out by counting words, types of word, phrases, repetitions, and so on. Thus, the overall boxing ambience of Text A(i) can be brought out by counting the words in List 4.2 and seeing what proportion of the total words in the passage they make up. They, in fact, account for 68 out of the 166 in the passage, roughly 40 per cent.

Counting can also reveal covert meanings of an ideological kind. An example of this is the way in which the commentator expresses enjoyment, satisfaction and approval of boxing, or at the progress of one boxer, perhaps Bruno, and how he builds on wider cultural assumptions about violence so that expressions of effective violence become terms of praise, and our approval of this is taken for granted. Consider the different terms used to express 'punch' as a noun in List 4.2:

(a) overhead right
(b) ramrod left jab
(c) left over the top
(d) scoring punch
(e) clubbing rights

There are no phrases in the quotation which give any evaluation. No 'good' or, as sometimes occurs, 'beautiful' punches are recorded, let alone 'brutal' or 'horrible' ones. Instead the commentator has an enthusiast's fascination with detail. Only in (d) is *punch* made explicit. Elsewhere the word *left* or *right* is used, leaving *punch* understood, as it will be by anyone familiar with boxing, but not by the outsider. Approval and enthusiasm are expressed (i) in the concentration on 'in' details, and (ii) on the very lack of evaluation, implying that there is no need for it. The examples listed are all phrases in which there are adjectives. But none of the adjectives is evaluative. They are all devoted to giving the enthusiastic listener the closest possible detail. This kind of point is worth bringing out because it reflects the conventions of this kind of text, and so of listeners' expectations. For these very reasons the patterning may not be immediately obvious to a listener. It just sounds normal.

We should perhaps add, in case it might appear that this analysis is aimed at devaluing boxing as a sport, that assumptions of normality and approval are common in very many kinds of text. The fact that such assumptions are implicit does not mean that they could not be explictly defended – in a different kind of text.

Another kind of patterning which can be brought out through counting is the tendency of the commentator not to use *is* and *he* when describing the boxing action. This kind of patterning we look at in Unit 5.

✎ EXERCISES

4.1 Text A(ii) in the appendix is a continuation of Text A(i). Make an analysis of the words in A(ii) along the lines of List 4.2. What proportion of the words are 'boxing words'?

4.2 Text D(i) is taken from a different kind of text, a narrative, and has a different kind of content, puppet making. Make a list of words or phrases which fit into the following types of patterning:

(a) puppet-making activities, including general words which have specifically puppet-making meanings here – show these in brackets: for example, *made* (carved);
(b) parts of the puppet/human body;
(c) time and sequence words or phrases such as *when, as soon as*;
(d) words expressing beginning and ending.

4.3 Most adult texts rely on the reader or listener's knowing something about the topic in hand. This itself produces word patterns made up of technical words, and of more common words used in specific ways affected by the particular context. Imagine we began to rewrite the boxing commentary in such a way that technical terms were explained for the beginner. Here is one example:

Original
Aims to throw an overhead right.

Rewriting
Aims to punch his opponent with his right gloved fist which is brought downwards from a position above his, the puncher's, head.

Comment on the value of technical words generally for a text, and for radio commentary in particular.

4.4 Text B covers the whole of the first round of the contest mentioned in Texts A(i–iii) but now as expressed in a television commentary.

   (a) Apply the same kind of analysis of types of words as was done in List 4.2.
   (b) What differences do you notice? Can you account for them in terms of the commentator's attitude?
   (c) What effect does the difference of medium have? Pick out one example where wording in quotations A(i) and B seems to you to have been affected by the medium.

PATTERNS OF GRAMMAR IN A TEXT

5

> The kind of words we will look at in this unit are words which are not associated with any particular kind of content or text; they are at home in any and every kind of text. They are very common words such as *is* and *he, the, but, of*. We will refer to them as function words.

The words we have discussed in previous units are, generally, associated with particular kinds of texts or topics. Such words are often referred to as CONTENT WORDS. Some of them are closely associated with particular contexts, for example *software* with computing, *referee* with sport, and so on. Typically, metaphor involves the translating of a word or a phrase from the types of text it is 'at home' in to one in which it is not usually used, as when *referee* is used of a marriage counsellor. Other words have a much wider range of application, but often have to be understood in particular ways in particular kinds of text, so that *delivery* is equally, but differently, 'at home' in the contexts of mail and childbirth.

Content words

FUNCTION WORDS are associated, not with any particular content, but with the grammar of English. They are the kinds of words that are difficult to pin down in dictionary definitions as 'referring' to something; and they fit into sets of words which have a relatively small number of members. One example of a set would be the *be* words we have mentioned, or the set of pronouns, *he, him, she, her, it, we, us, you, they, them*. To be able to speak the English language you have to know all of these words. Other kinds of words, the 'content' words, do not fit into limited sets like this. There is a vast number of words like *cat, table, happy, give*. You do not need to know all of these kinds of words to be able to speak English. Nobody knows every noun in English.

Function words

Although such words are ubiquitous in all texts, they do, in fact, figure in studies of style. Their interest to the student of style is the patterns they contribute to. For example, while almost any text will contain examples of the word *and*, there will often be significant differences in the pattern of use from one text to another.

Thus, when composing narratives, young children often say *and then ... and then* very many times. And usually, at the same time, other options for linking sentences are absent, for example by beginning, *furthermore* or *nevertheless*. And, when writing, young children are less likely to use linking words such as *when*, which involves making one clause subordinate to another.

To illustrate the point, here is an artificially simple piece of text in an *and ... and* style.

Style A: and ... and

Me and my friend went up the park and we went on the swings and we saw a dog and the dog was black, and we chased it and the dog went in a big house.

This could have been done differently by leaving out all the *and*s:

*Style B: no and*s

Me and my friend went up the park. We went on the swings. We saw a dog. The dog was black. We chased it. The dog went in a big house.

'A' and 'B' are made up and artificially simple and uniform, but they do illustrate the idea of stylistic pattern based on function words which shape grammatical structure. There is one overall tendency in A (to use nothing but *and* to link sentences), and another in B (never to use words like *and* to link sentences).

In real life things are never this simple, but we do find overall tendencies in texts, which depend on the writing taking the same kind of function word option, that is, the same grammatical option, a number of times.

Here are some examples.

Quotation 5.1

Coetzer the first man to come out with aggressive intent. Aims to throw an overhead right. But straight away Bruno flicking out that ramrod left jab. Coetzer slightly the taller man. Stands six foot four.

Quotation 5.2

After the eyes, he made the nose; but as soon as it was finished, it began to grow. It grew, and it grew, and in a few minutes' time it was as long as if there was no end to it. Poor Geppetto worked fast to shorten it.

Both passages represent a sequence of events in which there are actions being performed, fighting and carving. But there are differences in the way very common words such as *was* and *is* are used. Quotation 5.2, of course, is set in the past tense, so the word *was* occurs. Quotation 5.1 is set in the present, a 'blow-by-blow' account as it happens. So, in the following examples you might expect the word *is* to occur.

(1) Coetzer is the first man to come out . . .

(2) Bruno is flicking out that ramrod left jab.

(3) Coetzer is slightly the taller man.

But in A(i) it does not. Another function word difference is that 5.1 also sometimes does not use *he* or a name, where 5.2 does.
Compare (4) with (5):

(4) he made the nose
Poor Geppetto worked fast to shorten it.

(5) Aims to throw an overhead right.
Stands six foot four.

This kind of patterning interests students of style in two ways. The first is that the function word (or grammatical) patternings tend to be consistent throughout particular texts, and may be characteristic of them as types of text, or GENRES. We cannot be absolutely hard and fast, but we can say that it is typical of fiction to be expressed in the past tense, and commentaries in the present. It is also typical of commentaries to 'leave out' words such as *is* and *he*. Commentaries are, of course, spoken, and fiction is very often written, and hence composed at leisure as commentaries cannot be. Commentaries have a simple sentence patterning too, in the sense that there are relatively few words like *as soon as*, or *when*, which introduce dependent clauses.

Genres

In narrative fiction the writer maps out befores, and afters, and nexts, because he or she is inventing events happening in time. The commentator is also concerned with events happening in time, but more immediately, and cannot stand back and map befores and nexts from the global position of the fiction writer.

The style of the commentary is, in fact, not so distant from the *and . . . and* style. A large number of sentences do begin with *and*. The *and . . . and* style is much commoner in speech, and its occurrence in young children's writing is partly due to their writing much as they would speak.

A second point of interest for the student of style is that 5.1 is not different just from 5.2; it may appear to be 'odd' or 'deviant' in relation to the grammar of standard English. In that sense it is unconventional.

Stylistic patterning can usually be traced to the purposes of the speaker or writer, or to the cirumstances or medium in which they write or speak, or to conventions. But such purposes may not be obvious. Consider, for example, lack of *is* and *he* in passages of commentary (not in all passages, though). This may appear to be related to the need for the commentator to keep up with fast-moving events. But is this so? How much time is actually saved by saying (6) rather than (7)?

(6) Coetzer the first man.

(7) Coetzer's the first man.

Reasons are often difficult to establish in cases like this, but it could be that the lack of *is* and *he* may have a rhetorical rather than a time-saving basis, perhaps to give an impression of urgency. At all events, once the convention is established, commentators will tend to follow it. Although the grammar may not follow the rules of standard English it does follow the rules of commentary English.

Rather than attempting to describe differences of grammar associated with the common words we have been looking at, it is often more manageable to reshape passages in order to bring out these aspects of style. For example, how would the fiction look if it were 'translated' into commentary style?

Rewriting 5.1 Fiction to commentary

Geppetto making the eyes. Making the nose. Straightaway the nose starting to grow. Growing still. No end to it. Fast working from Geppetto. Tries to shorten it.

Immediately the passage begins to sound like some sort of competition, as if Geppetto were trying to make his puppet and control its nose faster than others. The blow-by-blow focus makes the writer sound as if he has not worked out what is to happen next, and that he is at the mercy of events rather than being the author who is inventing them, so he must focus on one at a time. One reason why the author of the original fictional passage is able to introduce dependent clauses beginning with such words as *as soon as* and *as if* is that he has a whole sequence of events in mind in advance. The commentator's relation to his subject matter also makes it difficult to accommodate *after*, and *in a few minutes* in the rewriting. The nearest phrase in the commentary is *straightaway*.

In rewriting the narrative we went some way beyond simply omitting *he* and *was*. But still, however hard we try, we cannot make the fiction passage sound convincing as a commentary, unless we conjure up a bizarre context such as a puppet-carving race. This discrepancy itself is informative and leads us back to the notion of conventions and expectations, which we discussed in Unit 2, and towards the connection between style, purpose and medium, which we look at in Unit 7.

EXERCISES ✎

5.1 Text E (in the appendix) comes from an essay by the naturalist Richard Jeffries. In this passage Jeffries uses forms of the verb *be* very frequently. By *be* words, I mean *be* itself and also *am*, *are*, *is*, *was*, *were*.

(a) How many *be* words are there altogether – that is, counting *be* and words such as *is*, *am*, *are*?

(b) Which is the commonest *be* word?

(c) Narratives are virtually impossible to write if you try to keep to *be* verbs only. In other words, they have a grammatical pattern that mirrors Jeffries' style in Text E. The pattern is for *be* words not very often to stand alone. Attempt to write the following made-up passage (which we used to illustrate the *and . . . and* pattern) replacing all the emphasised verbs by a *be* word whenever possible. You may alter word order and introduce place or time words such as *then* and *there*. For example, you might replace *we saw a dog* by *there was a dog*.

Me and my friend *went* up the park and we *went* on the swings and we *saw* a dog and the dog was black, and we *chased* it and the dog *went* in a big house.

(d) Why is it so difficult to turn some of the narrative verbs into *be* verbs?

5.2 In the passage by Richard Jeffries (Text E), there is another kind of function word patterning besides the use of *be* words. This is the use of words which deal with what is immediately present to the writer as he writes (if we can imagine him writing in the countryside). Note the following:

(a) expressions of the immediate context here and now;

(b) other words, less common than *is* or *now* etc., which refer to time; for example, the words *eternity*, and *years*.

Relate these patterns to:

(c) the explicit theme of the passage;

(d) the particular way Jeffries tries to persuade.

5.3 Text F in the appendix is taken from an interview given by Margaret Thatcher. Make a note of the number of times the following occur:

(a) you

(b) got to

(c) can, can't

(d) have to

Do you see any pattern of meaning uniting (a) – (d)?

5.4 Compare the grammatical patterning in the passages by Jeffries and Thatcher from the point of view of linking words. Note how many times the following are used in each text:

    (a) and
    (b) then
    (c) it
    (d) you

How might the differences in pattern here be connected to the difference in rhetorical purpose (and audience) of the two passages?

5.5 The study of stylistic patterning, which we have discussed in this unit, differs from some aspects of style studied in previous units in the sense that:

    (a) it is not usually self-conscious as, for example, the selection of a metaphor might be, or the choice of a *mot juste*, or flouting a convention;
    (b) it is relatively abstract and, when studied, statistical.

Discuss, if possible with others, what sorts of insight we gain by looking into grammatical patterning in texts, and types of text.

THE TEXTUAL ORCHESTRATION OF PATTERNS

6

In this Unit we will look at the way stylistic choices are orchestrated, that is, how the different patternings work together to give the text a distinctive stylistic 'grain'.

We begin with some further discussion of the passage by Richard Jeffries, which we discussed at the end of Unit 5. We have, in fact, already begun to see some orchestration. We noticed two kinds of patterning in Text E. There is the frequency of *be* verbs, and combined with it the tendency for sentences not to have linking words such as *and* or *when* or *therefore*. We will now develop this line of thought a little.

A further point to make about the *be* pattern is that much of its effect derives from the relative lack of other kinds of verb, in particular other kinds of verb that go next to *be*. The *be* words tend to stand by themselves in sentences such as *Eternity is now*. There are sixteen such free-standing *be* verbs. There are other verbs in the passage, one coming next to a *be* verb (*was raised*), the others free-standing (such as *floats*) or next to another word such as *has* or *may*. Of these other verbs there are nine. List 6.1 gives the phrases in which they occur, with the verbs themselves in emphasis.

List 6.1 Verbs other than free-standing be *verbs*

(1) *cannot understand* time

(2) the butterfly *floats*

(3) Nothing *has to come*

(4) I *exist* in it

(5) this tumulus *was raised*

(6) *is* mutually *agreed* on

(7) The shadow *goes*

(8) the index *moves*

(9) the clock *may make* time

These verbs are of different types, and do not in themselves form a pattern comparable in consistency to the free-standing *be* verbs.

The *be* verbs themselves are found as part of a slightly larger, grammatical, patterning. These verbs tend to be used with two broad kinds of meaning,

(a) defining: what time, eternity, etc. 'is';
(b) locating: where something is in either place or time.

Let us look first at (b). Here are some examples:

(10) It is eternity *now*

(11) I am *in the midst of it*

(12) It is about me *in the sunshine*

The emphasised phrases are all locative and refer to what the writer wants us to 'see' as being immediately present to him. This locative patterning is widespread. You will have an opportunity to see how widespread in Exercise 6.4. The locatives can be seen as part of the textual orchestration in that they chime in with the pervasive use of the present tense. Here are some examples of (a), the defining expressions:

(13) Now is *eternity*

(14) The years . . . are *absolutely nothing*

Together these defining *be* patterns also occupy a good deal of the text, which can be checked in detail in Exercise 6.4. They are all definitions and they are all assertions. They contribute to a pattern of assertive definitions given without linking words such as *because* or softening expressions such as *I think* or *possibly*.

The assertive definitions also form another kind of patterning connected to conventions, in particular the conventional meanings of words. Conventionally the word *eternity* does not mean 'now'. So when Jeffries asserts

(15) Now is eternity

he appears to be contradicting himself. What he is doing, of course, is challenging the received notions he assumes his readers have, about the meaning of *time* and *eternity*. He wants to locate them in an immediately present place, and to define them in a new way. One way of looking at this kind of patterning is to see it as a series of implicit denials of conventional wisdom as to what 'is', what is 'here' and what is 'now'.

Jeffries, like many poetic writers, wants us to challenge these every-day assumptions; and the challenge is articulated in the challenge to conventional 'making sense'.

Another kind of patterning is the repetition of words which are related in meaning to *time*, words such as *eternity*, *clock* and so on, and also words such as *it*, which refers frequently to *time*.

These 'time words' make up 20 per cent of the words in the passage. The proportion is higher if we count words which overlap *time* less fully in meaning: *dial*, *life* or, more tenuously, *tumulus*, and, more tenuously still, *butterfly*.

The repetition of time words contributes to two kinds of pattern: one is to do with the content of the passage, the continually mentioned idea of time; the other is the way in which repetition also serves to knit the text together. Jeffries uses repetition only to do this. He does not use sentence-linking words, which would produce a less 'stop–go' kind of flow to the text. His assertions are almost like a list. What connects them up is the continual reference to *time*. He is at the opposite extreme to the *and then . . . and then* style, and to the boxing commentary style. He is remote, too, from the argumentative sort of style which uses logical words such as *therefore*, *because*, *on the other hand*.

We have mentioned a number of different kinds of patterning:

(a) free-standing *be* verbs;
(b) present tense;
(c) *be* verbs followed by locative phrases;
(d) *be* verbs followed by definitions;
(e) unconventional word-meanings/assertions;
(f) repetition of time words;
(g) lack of sentence-connecting words.

The idea of stylistic 'orchestration' is the idea that these patterns reinforce each other. Everything comes back to the idea of 'being', of what 'is', to the idea of time, to the idea of what is immediately present here and now, and all these definitions and locations are very unconventional compared to the usual associations of words in English. This orchestration of words and meanings in relation to the central concept being put forward is matched by the stop–go sentences, without linking words to show how one follows from another, and without argument or justification.

The different patterns interact to give the text its particular 'grain'. At the same time there are aspects of it which might have been predicted: non-narrative texts tend to have a lot of *be* words in them; mystical and poetic texts tend to be assertive rather than logically argued.

This orchestration can be seen simply as the 'means to an end', 'how the language works', and little more than the consequence of the author's reason for writing.

Some students of style, however, might go further than this. For example, the assertive unconnected short present-tense sentences could be heard as an insistent hammering home of the point hammer-blow by hammer-blow. The writer states his definitions as if they were facts. He insists strongly on them, one after another. This is strange, it might seem, in a text which is so very subjective. There is no *I believe, so it seems to me, I feel.* Perhaps – one of these more adventurous commentators might claim – this reflects a conflict some-where 'behind' the text, the assertiveness being a way in which the author refuses to acknowledge that his subjective speculations about time are less than certain truths.

Other writers treat this kind of comment with some scepticism; but to write it off completely as mere speculation begs a question as to 'where' the meaning of the text lies. There are writers who would say that, to an extent at least, the meaning and rhetorical effect is 'in our-selves'.

Another approach, which also raises this question, would be to look at the strange fact that the word *is* in English does not necessarily indicate present time just because we name it present tense. It often indicates a 'timeless' present, especially when used in definitions. Is it this, then, that Jeffries is exploiting in saying that timeless eternity is 'now' in the present? If so, could it be that Jeffries reveals not some idiosyncratic view of his own but a paradox in the way our language has evolved? In the end he is saying something about how we talk about time and eternity rather than time and eternity themselves. But then, how do we distinguish what time 'is' from how we define it?

Let us look at a different kind of text, the boxing commentary. Here the description and the rhetorical purposes of the speaker, as well as the genre, are quite different. Look again at Text A(i) in the appendix. The verbs which fit the context of boxing particularly closely tend to be of two types:

(a) verbs describing an unfinished try at something, such as *aims to throw, flicking out, trying to land*;
(b) verbs describing the successful achievement of something, such as *got Bruno backed up, thudded into*.

These are all action verbs as opposed to the categorising verbs in Jeffries. Action verbs make different grammatical demands from categorising verbs. The action verb requires the speaker to state who is the actor and who is the receiver of the action, in this case, mainly, the punches. In boxing this is a crucial point. But Jeffries' text (Text E) does not require that sort of stylistic decision. There are no actions.

The aspects of grammatical style we have looked at are very clearly connected both with the content of the texts concerned and with the writer's or speaker's purposes in writing or speaking. There is a parallel of a kind between sentence structure and what we might call **Content structure**   CONTENT STRUCTURE. The *be* words mime the philosophical defin-ing and locating Jeffries is trying to establish; the *try/succeed/punch* words reflect the physical interaction the commentator describes.

Both texts aim to produce a sense of immediacy, but one is an immediacy of awareness (eternity is here and now), and another an immediacy of description (the contest is happening here and now).

Also both texts lack what we might call 'back-up' The events come rushing in on the commentator. He has just the odd moment to fill us in about the background, or to select what is crucial for the fight as a whole. And Jeffries makes no attempt to give a logical back-up or justification for his assertions. There are no *because* or *therefore* links in his text as there might be if he were writing in a logical philosophical way.

6.1 Pick out all the words or phrases in Text A(i), which contain the meaning 'punch', whether as a noun (*a punch*) or as a verb (*punching*, *punches* etc.). How are these like, and also unlike, the 'time' words in Text E?

6.2 Go through Text A(i) and pick out all the words or phrases which indicate the immediate here and now. How do they differ from the expressions of the immediate here and now in the passage from Richard Jeffries?

6.3 Give examples of the following patterns in Text D in the appendix:

    (a) time sequence words or phrases (e.g. *as soon as*);
    (b) words standing for carving and making;
    (c) words standing for the body (do not include *it*);
    (d) words such as *start, finish*;
    (e) patterns of repeated events;
    (f) any word patterns you have noticed not so far mentioned.

In what ways would you say that these patterns reinforce each other?

6.4 Complete the following list of locative expressions from Text E, which all begin with a preposition.

    in the midst
    about me
    in the sunshine
    in it
    in the light-laden air . . .

    (a) Is there a pattern within this pattern? For example, are certain words particularly common?
    (b) There are other phrases beginning with prepositions which are not locative (indicating time or place) These are:

for the clock

for itself

for me

Make any comment you think relevant about these and how they contrast with all the other prepositional phrases in the text, and what *for the clock* and *for itself* mean literally.

(c) We mentioned that some stylisticians are more speculative than others. Would you attach any significance to the use of the preposition *in* in the locative phrases? What meanings does it have in these? Look back at Unit 3 and consider whether *in* in Text E might be metaphorical.

THE EFFECTS OF THE MEDIUM

7

The medium of expression affects the style of a text. This may be a matter of conventions of politeness or layout, as in a business letter, or of constraints made by the channel of communication — such as not being able to use intonation in written texts.

Style is always to some extent shaped by and stimulated by the medium used by the writer or speaker. Speaking provides slightly different contraints and opportunities from writing. Postcards, inscriptions on rings or gravestones, headlines and slogans affect style because of the limited physical space they allow. Television commentary gives rise to a slightly different style from radio commentary, different again from newspaper reporting. When we write a small ad to sell our car the cost per word makes for economy of expression. We write

   (1) Car for sale.

leaving out function words, rather than

   (2) I have a car for sale.

Instructions written on such things as fire extinguishers are constrained by space too. We find

   (3) Stand on table.

rather than

   (4) Stand the extinguisher on the table.

   Another example of constraint by the medium is verse. Usually, in English, verse requires a set number of syllables per line. These also, usually, have to follow the pattern of alternate stress and unstress:

35

di	DUM	di	DUM	di	DUM	di	DUM
A	vintage		M	G	sports	for	sale.
In	perfect		nick	from	nose	to	tail.

You will notice that the constraint has positive aspects. It makes the wording sound neat, and may suggest a humorous and approachable seller, easy to deal with.

The examples we have considered so far have been illustrative and clearcut. Let us consider some less simple examples. We will look at the whole of Text A, which is made up of texts A(i), (ii) and (iii), at Text B, the television commentary, and also the part of a report of the fight, Text C, covering the same three minutes of the contest.

There are a number of points of difference among these three texts. Let us confine ourselves to three:

(a) length in words;
(b) *be* words;
(c) linking words.

LENGTH

The two spoken passages are the same length in minutes, because they run alongside the events described, and these take place in the final two minutes of the first round of the contest. But the length on the page, as words, is different. Text A has 525 words in it, and Text B, 143. This difference is directly connected to the medium since the television commentator does not have to represent in words what the viewers can see for themselves. This means that the television commentator's role is slightly different from the radio commentator's, and can be seen much more as that of giving expert footnotes to what is going on. The radio commentator does this too, but must also describe things the listener cannot see. Hence he talks a lot more.

The radio commentator, however, cannot hope to cover every single blow and movement, especially in so fast a sport as boxing. So he must select quite drastically so as give, not every single blow, but an impression of the way things are going. He must also try to give a relatively objective viewpoint, for example by mentioning each boxer by name the same number of times (19 times), while at the same time bearing in mind that most of his listeners will want Bruno to win. So things will tend to be seen from the viewpoint of his prospects, as is shown by the commentator's reference to *the South African* for Coetzer, but not *the Englishman* for Bruno (the television commentator at one point refers to Bruno as *Frank*).

The report is different because it is a summary written after the bout. The reporter has had time to reflect and pick out what were the turning points and important moments. His selection is thus the more considered, though very similar to the commentator's in content.

We noticed how the radio commentator tended sometimes not to put in *be* words and also *he* or the names of boxers, and sometimes other words which we would expect in standard English. This gives an impression of immediacy. The television commentator does not do this, except at one point towards the end, where he says.

> Coetzer [is] being clubbed to the head. [he] Didn't even flinch. But once again Bruno [is] told by Roy Francis not to hold. Coetzer [attacks] with a little flurry.

Apart from this passage he uses the full standard English forms. In general his style is relaxed, standing back, passing knowledgeable remarks on the events. This relaxed tone does not come out in a transcription where the relatively long silences are not reproduced.

Mee's report, of course, includes the *be* words throughout, but in the past tense, which also gives a greater sense of distance, and also a sense of completedness. His role is to produce not a sense of immediacy but considered reflection.

Another difference between the television and radio commentaries is that the television commentator is much less inclined than the radio commentator to begin sentences with *and*. In Text A 40 per cent of the sentences begin with an *and* or a *but*, whereas in Text B only 13 per cent do. These figures are cited to illustrate a method used in the study of style, but in this case they are not too meaningful because the passages are so short. To establish the point fully much longer passages would have to be analysed. This difference in the use of *and* or *but* is probably due to the fact that the radio commentator has that much less time to consider his words than the television commentator does.

A complication to the point is that *sentence* is difficult to define in an oral text. I have based it on intonation. There are other *and*s and *but*s in A(i), which occur within (intonationally defined) sentences, of course.

The television commentator, however, does use the rather different linking word *although* (twice), while the radio commentator does not use any linking word like this. Its function is to make sentences longer, so that they have one clause dependent on another. Compare the following. The radio commentator uses two simple sentences to mention the men's heights:

> (5) Coetzer slightly the taller man. Stands six foot four.

The television commentator uses a single sentence with a dependent clause beginning with *although*:

> (6) Bruno has quite a lot of reach advantage, although Coetzer is actually an inch taller.

And a little later there is another *although* clause from the television commentator:

> (7) Although Bruno weighs this massive seventeen stone six he still looks quite lively on his feet.

The sentence structures in the report reflect the need for the reporter to condense, and also the fact that he has had time to plan his wording. The events are not crowding in on him as he writes. So he can come up with quite complex sentences such as:

> (8) Bruno had to absorb a cracking left hook, landed a thumping overhand right, but then had to give ground as Coetzer got through with his share of blows in a hard, close first round.

He saves himself having to repeat *Bruno* or *he* by making the first mention serve the first three verbs (*had to absorb*, *landed* and *had to give*) and he can make events which happened several minutes apart flow into one sentence. The commentator cannot do this because he cannot see the outcome of the series of events as they are happening.

Sentence (8) can be seen as a weaving together of the following simpler sentences:

> Bruno had to absorb a cracking left hook.
>
> Bruno landed a thumping overhand right.
>
> But Bruno then had to give ground.
>
> Coetzer got through with his share of blows.
>
> It was a hard close first round.

The report, of course, is in a written medium which allows the writer to cross things out and experiment with drafts until satisfied. The commentator has to compose on his feet, and mention things before their outcomes are apparent. Also, the *and ... and* form is characteristic of spoken language, the use of dependent structures typical of economical planned writing.

DENSITY

A very important difference between most spoken and most written texts is the relatively greater density of meaning the latter tends to have. This is because in speech we tend to use proportionately more words like *and, he, as, for, be, on* and so on than we do when we write. For example, the proportion of function words in Text G in the appendix – a rhetorical speech – is roughly 54 per cent, whereas the proportion in Text D – a written children's story – is about 44 per cent.

Lexical density

The density of content words, more usually called LEXICAL DENSITY, for each text is expressed as the proportion of words which are *not* the function type. So the lexical density of the speech is 46 per cent, while that of the written children's story is 56 per cent.

This reflects, in part, the difference between written and spoken language, though often spoken language is much less dense than this. We must bear in mind the particular professional skill of commentators to make their speech relatively more dense and information-packed than casual conversation would be.

✐ **EXERCISES**

7.1 Go through Text A(i–iii) and Text B, and list for each one:

  (a) the average number of words per sentence;
  (b) the proportion of *and*s and *but*s in each text; this time, not only those at the beginnings of orthographic sentences;
  (c) the proportion of *be* words in each text; count also abbreviated versions of these, as in *he's*;
  (d) the proportion of 'spaces' where there would be a *be* or *he* or some other word in standard English;

Comment on any unexpected results, and suggest possible reasons for them.

7.2 Compare the lexical density of the following passages, headed Quotations 7.4–7 below. The function words are capitalised (including *I*). Each passage is exactly fifty words long.

  (a) Put the quotations in order from lowest to highest lexical density.
  (b) Bearing in mind that such small quotations are not really reliable as a basis for generalisations, nevertheless suggest a reason why the least dense text is least dense.
  (c) Suggest a reason, to do with the medium, for the difference between the two versions of the *Pinocchio* story.
  (d) Suggest a reason, to do with the medium and the type of text it is, for the most dense passage being most dense.

Quotation 7.4

I believe THAT government SHOULD BE VERY strong TO DO THOSE things WHICH ONLY government CAN DO. IT HAS TO BE strong TO HAVE defences, BECAUSE THE kind OF Britain I see WOULD ALWAYS defend ITS freedom AND ALWAYS BE A reliable ally. SO YOU'VE GOT TO BE strong . . .

Quotation 7.5

IT IS undoubtedly THE case THAT THE sciences ARE organized bodies OF knowledge AND THAT IN ALL OF THEM A classification OF THEIR materials INTO significant types OR kinds (AS IN biology, THE classification OF living things INTO species) IS AN indispensable task. IT IS clear, NONETHELESS, THAT THE proposed . . .

E. Nagel (1979) *The Structure of Science: Problems in the Logic of Scientific Explanation* (London: Routledge), p. 3

Quotation 7.6

HAVING thought OUT A name FOR HIS puppet, HE started HIS work WITH great determination. HE made HIS hair, HIS forehead, AND HIS eyes IN A VERY short time.

AS SOON AS THE eyes WERE finished, imagine HIS bewilderment WHEN HE saw THEM moving AND looking AT HIM. WHEN Geppetto . . .

Quotation 7.7

Geppetto THE wood carver lived IN A little wooden house WITH HIS cat, Figaro, AND A goldfish called Cleo. HE made lots OF marvellous toys, BUT HE HAD NO children TO play WITH THEM.

ONE day HE made A puppet FROM SOME pine wood, AND put strings ON IT, SO . . .

SEQUENCES OF WORDS AND EVENTS

8

This unit deals with the sequence in which we mention things in a text as a whole, or in a paragraph, and in the wording of individual sentences, and how this may create emphasis, or surprise.

Just as a writer must make choices as to the exact words and phrases to use, choosing between similar alternatives, such as *sofa* and *settee*, or between different focuses on the same content, such as *car* or *wheels* or *MG*, so too he or she must make choices about the sequence in which words, phrases, sentences and ideas are to occur. Perhaps the most striking example of this comes from stories where there is a flashback. This is a stylistic option in the sense that the 'same' narrative may be told in a different sequence. Take *Jack and the Beanstalk*. We could start:

> *Opening 1*
> Once upon a time there was a poor widow and her son Jack . . .

and then follow through the story in the same sequence as the imaginary events occur. Or we could start

> *Opening 2*
> One morning Jack woke up and saw a huge beanstalk outside his bedroom window.

and then explain its presence by going back over what had happened the day before.

The flashback version is the more immediately exciting because it begins with the extraordinary beanstalk, and then prompts questions in the reader's mind. On the other hand, it is that much more difficult to understand a story which is told out of ordinary sequence, because the sequence of events does not now match the sequence of sentences. The flashback would be less likely in a story written for children, with less experience of narrative and of sorting out a sequence of events.

The flashback also poses problems for the narrator in filling in essential information needed by the reader to make sense of the story, the so-called 'exposition'. Opening 1 begins with exposition, introducing the characters and their situation; opening 2 still has all this to do. The wording of any continuation of opening 2 will show this, because the narrator will have to use words like *before that* and use, for example, *had gone to the market, had met, had sold*, where opening 1 will require *went, met* and *sold*.

The flashback is striking because it flouts what seems the most 'natural' sequencing: that is, making language events follow the same sequence as events in the story. It is less conventional and that much less expected.

A different kind of 'natural' sequence is imposed by some kinds of argument-based texts which make the sequence of language follow the sequence of the argument. Here is a figure and a passage from a textbook on elementary geometry. It refers to the following figure:

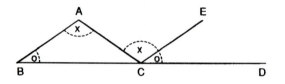

Proof

(1) AB and CE are parallels and AC is a transversal.
      ∴ Alternate angles ACE, BAC are equal.

(2) AB and CE are parallel and BC is a transversal.
      ∴ Corresponding angles ECD, ABC are equal.

(3) By addition:
      $\angle BAC + \angle ABC = \angle ACE + \angle ECD = \angle ACD$

Source: Abbott, P. (1970) *Teach Yourself Geometry* (Kent: Hodder & Stoughton).

Although it seems most natural to follow this sequence, making statements followed by *therefore*, the passage could be taken in the reverse sequence, starting with the last statement and then working back by saying *because* each time. Consider (1) and (2):

(1) This is a posh store. Therefore the things are expensive here.

(2) The things are expensive here because this is a posh store.

Sometimes sequence may be almost wholly a matter of how the speaker handles an audience, for example in a teacher's decision as to where to begin an explanation of how flaps work on a paper glider. The ideas themselves do not impose a 'natural' sequence. So the teacher could begin by demonstrating a glider flight with the flaps in an upturned position and say:

(3) What made it climb rather than dive?

Or they might begin with the question

(4) What will make it climb rather than dive?

and do the demonstration afterwards to test the answers. Or they might start by asking for a definition:

(5) What do flaps do?

The meditation by Jeffries (Text E) is another example of a text in which the sequence of ideas is very much a matter of presentation. But although it is neither logical nor narrative, it does work by beginning with what will be most familiar to the reader and moves towards what will be unfamiliar, the idea that there is no time.
Here is the opening of the passage.

Quotation 8.1

I cannot understand time. It is eternity now. I am in the midst of it. It is about me in the sunshine; I am in it, as the butterfly floats in the light-laden air. Nothing has to come; it is now. Now is eternity; now is the immortal life.

We can, in fact, write the sentences (and parts of sentences marked by commas and semi-colons) in reverse order and still make sense.

Rewriting of quotation 8.1

Now is the immortal life. Now is eternity; it is now. Nothing has to come; it is now. As the butterfly floats in the light-laden air, I am in it; it is about me in the sunshine. I am in the midst of it. It is eternity now. I cannot understand time.

Sense of a kind, but not quite the same sense. For one thing it is made much more mysterious by starting with *now* and the startling notion 'Now is the immortal life', rather than leading up to it. In 8.1 the idea of 'now' had been connected to ideas already mentioned, and questions already posed. Jeffries had already said that he cannot understand time and that for him eternity is now. None of this preparation has been done for us in the reversed version. We start with the very startling remark about now and then get the reasoning as we go on, very much as if we were to read the theorem backwards, or started with the flashback in a story.

The sequencing of a text, then, has to do with the way we handle the reader's or listener's understanding. How far do we plunge in with new unexplained things? How far do we fill in what we understand that the reader will need to know if they are to grasp the new material or striking events we want to bring in? Do we start with background information and lead up to new information? Or do we start with new information and pose questions in the reader's or listener's mind about it, and then begin to answer those questions?

What has been said about sequencing so far is connected to the following and flouting of conventions, and conventional expectations, which we looked at in Unit 2.

Another way of looking at sequence as an aspect of style is to look at the ways in which a speaker or writer creates a continuous thread of meaning running through a text, how one thing leads to another. We have seen how *it* takes us back to previously mentioned *eternity*. This *it* is very common through the whole text, and serves to connect it up. Each *it* (until we get to 'it is only a moment', where a different kind of *it* occurs) takes us back to the previous one, and eventually back to *time*. The same point can be made about the repetitions of *I* and in a slightly different way *is*.

All texts have these kinds of threads of continuity. The point to be made from the point of view of style is that there are different options open to a writer or speaker as to how such cohesion is achieved. The many examples of *I* and *is* attest to the short sentences, each requiring an *I* and an *is*. Jeffries might have written in longer sentences. He might have deployed linking words like *and* and *but*, *nevertheless*, *when*:

> (6) It is eternity now – which I am in the midst of and which is about me in this sunshine I am in, as the butterfly . . .

instead of the 'stop–start' style of sentences he does use.

Again, instead of repeating *it*, he could have gone for a different kind of emphasis by saying *eternity* over and over again:

> (7) It is eternity now. I am in the midst of eternity. Eternity is about me in the sunshine. I am in eternity as the butterfly floats in the . . .

Another option would have been to find words with a strong overlap of meaning with *eternity* and used them:

> (8) It is eternity now. I am in the midst of timelessness. The everlasting is about me in the sunshine. I am in the infinite as the butterfly floats in the . . .

Or he could have used *and* before every sentence. And so on.

So far we have looked at sequence from the point of view of whole texts or longish passages. The same sorts of options face the composer in the small scale too.

Consider the following combinations of the same words as possible openings for *Jack and the Beanstalk*:

> (9) Once there was a poor widow

(10) There was once a poor widow

(11) There was a poor widow once

(12) A poor widow, there was, once

(13) A poor widow once there was

Changing the sequence of words and phrases like this affects the rhetorical effect rather than the narrative content. But it is quite difficult to pin down exactly what the differences are. This is because it would be possible to read aloud the same words in different ways, and so impose personal interpretations which might differ subtly from person to person.

Nevertheless we can say that as we go down the list from (9) to (12) the tone a reader would be most likely to give the words gets less formal, and that, as an opening, (13) would most likely occur as part of a song or rhyme.

Examples (9), (10) and (11) differ in the placing of *once*. Example (9) is most clearly fairy story language where *once* leads the way and provides the time frame for what follows. The first word announces 'This is a children's narrative.' In this sense it prompts the most formal kind of delivery. Examples (10) and (11) would be more likely in a conversation or some other kind of genre than would (9), and you may feel that (11), where *once* is added on at the end, is that much less formal than (10). In (9) and (10) it is quite easy to say *once* with a high pitch; but this is not nearly so easy with (11). And in (12) the words *there was, once* sound like 'throw-away lines' imitating unplanned conversation, as if *there was, once* came as an afterthought while the person was speaking. It would, in fact, with good acting, be possible to say (13) also in this throw-away style.

Examples (9)–(13) represent very small-scale differences, and taking them apart in this way may seem over-precise. The point to remember is that such small-scale (usually unconsciously made) choices accumulate in a text to give it the 'grain' we discussed when we looked at the orchestration of patterns in Unit 6. When we look at these small-scale choices of wording in the wider context of a text as a whole, and so see a pattern, accounting for their rhetorical effect can often be less tenuous. Nevertheless the discussion of (9)–(13) does raise the question as to how far discussion of stylistic 'effect' is a subjective matter. There is a chance to look at this further in Exercise 8.4 below.

━━━━━━━━━━━━━━━━━━━━━━━━━━━━━━━━━━   ✐ **EXERCISES**

8.1 The following passages represent two possible openings for *Jack and the Beanstalk*. Opening (B) is the more conventional, and the story could be begun simply by tacking (A) onto (B). But what happens if you start with (A) and then tack on (B)?

Make an opening like this, starting with (A) and then adapting (B) but keeping as close to the original wording as you can.

(a) What are the most important kinds of alteration you have
   had to make?
(b) What are the main advantages and disadvantages of each
   approach?

Opening (A)

As soon as he woke up he felt that there was something
strange, something about the light. Everything seemed a
weird green. He got out of bed, went over to the window
and drew back the curtain. His mouth fell open. There,
right in front of the window, blocking the whole sky was
an absolutely vast plant. What was it? Where had it come
from? Then he remembered yesterday.

Opening (B)

There was once a widow and her son Jack who lived on a
farm. They were so poor that one day, his mother said to
Jack, 'Jack, take the cow to the market and sell her.' So he
did. But on the way he met a man who said, 'Look, I'll give
you these magic beans for that cow of yours. They're worth
more than money could buy.' So Jack took the beans.
   His mother was furious and flung the beans out of the
window and sent Jack to bed. The next morning . . .

8.2 Text G is taken from a history of the Native Americans. Part of
its rhetorical effect is the way in which the composer creates
sequences of the same kind of sentence.

(a) Pick out sentences, or parts of sentences which have a
   similar sequence of words, such as *I was born*, or *I lived*.
(b) Make a list of:

   (i) each word which occurs immediately before either a
      full stop or a comma, and refers to natural life of the
      prairie; this list will start *prairie, sun*, etc.
   (ii) each word which occurs immediately before either a
      full stop or a comma, and refers to restrictions. This will
      start *reservation, lodges*, etc.

(c) List the first three words of each sentence.
(d) What pattern do you see to the way these beginnings and
   endings are handled?

8.3 Look at these three versions of a passage from Text G. For each
one discuss:

(a) What stylistic alterations have been made?
(b) What differences are produced in shades of meaning or
   rhetorical effect?

Version 1

Where the wind blew free and there was nothing to break the light of the sun, I was born. Where there were no enclosures and where everything drew a free breath, I was born.

Version 2

I was born where there were no enclosures and there was nothing to break the light of the sun. I was born upon the prairie, where the wind blew free and where everything drew a free breath.

Version 3

I was born upon the prairie; I was born where the wind blew free; and I was born where there was nothing to break the light of the sun. I was born where there were no enclosures; and I was born where everything drew a free breath.

8.4 This activity involves a more socially orientated kind of research. Ideally the best results would be obtained if you could question a large number of people, not necessarily people interested in style, or other academic topics. But you can get an idea of the way possibly subjective assessments might be tested if you work with one or two other people who are studying this book.

(a) Taking examples (9)–(13) above, make your own judgements as to the ways they differ from each other in rhetorical effect, or in finer shades of meaning.
(b) Compare your judgements with those of at least one other person. Is there any consistency? If so, what? If not, what conclusion do you draw?

9 THE SELECTION OF SIGNIFICANT DETAIL

> Another aspect of style is selection of significant detail. Given a particular scene or event what do we make explicit about it and what do we leave 'understood'?

There is a sense in which selection forms the basis of any text. The most straightforward way to see this is when we describe what is before our eyes. How would you describe the room you are in now?

In theory you could go on mentioning details for ever: every speck of dust, or dimple in the wallpaper, is 'there'. But you will not mention 'everything', and will not need to. A few details will do, and then you can leave it to the reader's experience to fill in the rest. The trick is to make the details that you do choose 'call up' the whole scene or situation. This is what is meant by their being 'significant'.

In the boxing commentary the commentator is constrained also by the medium. He does not have time to mention many details. He selects key items for mention in order to create an impression of the whole scene. In the radio commentary the commentator does not mention every blow, but picks out samples, so that we have the impression that Coetzer is doing more attacking. A specimen number of key incidents stands in for the whole. Of course this requires judgement and knowledge from the commentator, as can be appreciated if we imagine someone with no knowledge of boxing being given the job of describing it. They would not know even what was significant to pick out for mention, let alone terms such as

    (1) right over the top

which allow the commentator to be concise.

The technique of using a part to stand for the whole applies to details as well as overall strategy. Thus in Text G Parra-Wa-Same picks out for mention 'every stream and every wood'. Obviously he knew other things as well, such as ponds, fish, teepees, eagles, his family, and so forth. Jeffries (Text E), also, makes use of particular parts of the setting. His whole thesis is that part and whole are contained in each other.

> (2) It [eternity] is about me in the sunshine; I am in it, as the butterfly floats in the light-laden air.

He selects some parts of the whole but not others. He might have mentioned the moonlight, and the moth floating in a star-laden dark.

Sometimes, selection can be used as a way of producing an 'in' style which will not be understood by outsiders. It is this kind of selection, with a different purpose, that forms the basis of riddles. With a riddle details are selected in such a way as to be accurate but also idiosyncratic, that is, not significant as a clue to calling up the whole.

Mentioning a part or parts to suggest the whole is not the only kind of selection. Sometimes we mention, not a part, but a specific type of something. As has already been mentioned, a 'right over the top' is a type of punch. To understand it we have to be able to grasp that the phrase contains the meaning *punch*, just as mentioning *Volvo* or *Ford* in a small ad contains the meaning 'car'.

Being able to select is a key skill for the fiction writer. Here are the two versions of the *Pinocchio* story adapted for young children and based on Walt Disney's film. In them the writers have told the same story, but have made different selections.

The two versions differ in that the one is written as a Ladybird story book, and the other a pamphlet to go with an audio tape. The tape has the character of Jiminy Cricket as first-person narrator. In each, selection is used to give a different angle on the imaginary events.

Quotation 9.1

Geppetto the wood carver lived in a little wooden house with his cat, Figaro, and a goldfish called Cleo. He made lots of marvellous toys, but he had no children to play with them.

One day he made a puppet from some pine wood, and put strings on it so that it could dance. He called the puppet Pinocchio.

> (taken from Text D(ii) in the appendix)

Quotation 9.2

Have you ever wondered if wishes really do come true? Well, they do! And I, Jiminy Cricket, have seen it happen! Here, let me tell you about it.

One starry night my travels took me to a tiny shop owned by Geppetto the woodcarver.

I sneaked under the door and saw old Geppetto working on a puppet that looked like a little boy. Geppetto put on

a last dab of paint and said, 'There, little woodenhead,
you're all finished! Now, I have just the name for you –
Pinocchio!'

(taken from Text D(iii) in the appendix)

Quotation 9.2 is less 'natural' in the sense that it does not take the
story step by step as 9.1 does. In 9.1 Geppetto, his house and his pets
are all announced as a starting point. The scene is set first. Now we
can move into what happens. Quotation 9.2 is not like this. First
Jiminy Cricket discusses the overall theme of wishing and how he has
proved it works, introduces himself as a wanderer and then in a kind
of flashback, gives the Pinocchio story as an example of that.

We have basically 'the same' Walt Disney version of Collodi's
rather different original, but with different things selected for mention, or nonmention.

In 9.2 more words are given to Jiminy and there is dialogue. In 9.1
we have:

(3) He called the puppet Pinocchio.

in 9.2:

(4) 'There, little woodenhead, you're all finished! Now,
I have just the name for you – Pinocchio!'

The dialogue is introduced so as to give scope, on the tape, for voice
acting, and introduces the endearment *little woodenhead* with a young
listener in mind. The requirements of the medium – taped acting with
plenty of 'warm feeling' – affect the selection here.

There is another sense in which the medium affects selection
too. That is that both texts must be short enough to encourage
children to read them. Quotation 9.2 as a whole is shorter than 9.1
but has the same story to tell. The decision to spend more words on
the character of Jiminy means that words have to be saved elsewhere.
This is mainly in the narrative passages: for example, 9.1 tells us
Geppetto has no child and mentions both a goldfish and a cat. 9.2
mentions only one of these, the cat.

Differences of selection can be seen in the more subtle aspects of
wording, also, for example in the different ways in which Geppetto's
home is presented:

(5) *from 9.1*   *from 9.2*

little   tiny

wooden   –

house   shop

And in 9.2 (from Text D(iii)) 'Geppetto' becomes 'old Geppetto',
an example of the tendency of 9.2 to select for wording with the
expression of somewhat cosy sentiment in mind.

Geppetto himself is the main focus in 9.1 (from Text D(ii)),
who he is and where he lives. He is, at that point, the main person in
the story. But in 9.2 he is not. His 'tiny shop' is mentioned only as

part of the experience of Jiminy. The tiny shop is focused on as part of 'where my travels took me', and Geppetto as the content of what Jiminy saw. This is a matter of sentence structure as the sentences are shaped so that 'to a tiny shop' and 'old Geppetto' are given a passive role in relation to 'my travels' and what 'I saw'.

It may not be apparent that 'my travels took me', is a grammatical type of metaphor. Literally it is people who go on travels, not the reverse. The wording sounds as if travels were causes rather than the medium of Jiminy's movements. For younger children this kind of metaphor will be more difficult to interpret than the simpler head-on announcement in 9.1, in which the option of metaphor is not taken. As often happens, it seems as if the adult attempt to 'talk down' to children has in fact made things more problematic for them.

Selection is, of course, related to ideological presuppositions about the topic and the reader or listener and their relation to the writer or speaker, here between the writer and a child reader, as to what sorts of stories are suitable for children, what sorts of stories they like, what sorts of morals the text should exemplify, for example about cheekiness and lying.

✎ EXERCISES

9.1 Items (i)–(viii) consist of words used to describe, the entities described being given in parentheses. How do the descriptions work? For each one, decide whether it is

  (a) by mention of the part to stand for the whole;
  (b) by mention of a member to stand for the category;
  (c) by mention of the whole to stand for the part;
  (d) by mention of the category to stand for a member;
  (e) by mention of a member of one category to stand for a member of another (metaphor).

  (i)   wheels (car)
  (ii)   artillery (revolver)
  (iii) in black and white (published)
  (iv)   the feline (tiger)
  (v)   on his feet (making a speech)
  (vi)   a V neck (sweater)
  (vii) she wears the trousers (she dominates)
  (viii) goddesses (Hollywood actresses)

9.2 Compare the passages below. Try to pinpoint exactly what the differences are, and if you can, make some comments about what effect they have on nuances of meaning. Make two columns in which the same events are represented by slightly different selections of detail in wording, for example, as we noticed in Quotations 9.1 and 9.2:

9.1	9.2
little wooden house	tiny shop

Pinocchio A

When he went to bed that night, Geppetto looked out and saw the bright Evening Star shining in the sky. 'Look!' he said to Figaro, 'It's a wishing star!'
    So Geppetto made a special wish,

> I wish I may, I wish I might
> Have the wish I wish tonight!

His secret wish was that little Pinocchio might become a real boy!

(from Text D(ii))

Pinocchio B

Just before going off to sleep, Geppetto looked out of his window into the starry night. 'Oh, look, Figaro! The Wishing Star! Do you know what I wish, Figaro? I wish that my little Pinocchio might become a real boy!'

(from Text D(iii))

9.3

Personal advertisement

Strict lady wishes to contact gents, who would like to visit a formally dressed governmess [*sic*] or headmistress (black stockings, academic gown etc.). Or I could be your aunt, matron, nanny etc. I correct faults using traditional discipline. Sub ladies also welcome. Unhurried. Sussex Coast. letterbox no . . .

(Text H in the appendix)

Comment on the critera for selection here from the point of view of:

(a) what is, and is not, mentioned;
(b) the pattern created by the selections of *strict lady, governess, headmistress, aunt, matron, nanny*;
(c) words with the category meaning of 'communication' used for one particular kind of communication.

9.4 This is a riddle. Suggest some solutions, and discuss how selection here is used to deceive, by presenting something from a very idiosyncratic or nonsignificant angle. What are the strategies?

I overflow with words. My cap goes on my bottom.

The solution is given at the end of this unit.

9.5 Make your own analysis of the differences in selection in the following passages. If you can, comment on any overall differences between the texts, and possible motivations for them (for example, to do with the medium, writer's purposes, audience envisaged, space available).

Pinocchio C

At that moment the room where Pinocchio lay began to fill with dazzling bright light. Out of the light stepped the Blue Fairy of the Evening Star, who had heard Geppetto's secret wish. The fairy waved her wand over Pinocchio, saying,

'Little puppet, made of pine,
Wake! The gift of life is thine!'

(from Text D(ii))

Pinocchio D

Moments later the room filled with light, and there stood a beautiful Blue Fairy. She tapped Pinocchio with her magic wand.

'Little puppet made of pine –
wake! the gift of life is thine.

(from Text D(iii))

Solution to the riddle: pen or biro.

10 PERSONAL ATTITUDE, INVOLVEMENT AND EMOTION

> In this unit we look at the ways in which the attitude of the speaker or writer gets into the verbal structures he or she uses, their emotional involvement or detachment, their point of view and ideology.

Referring to the same individual, one person might say *lout* or *yobbo* or *hooligan*, while someone else might say *demonstrator* or *protester*, or perhaps *activist*. These are differences in selection of words, of course, and a difference in selection of details being highlighted; but they also reveal differences in attitude, emotional colouring, personal involvement, and general forcefulness. This sort of difference we will call a difference of 'tenor'. We have already mentioned some aspects of tenor in talking about conventions in Unit 2. Saying

(1) Respected Sir

as opposed to

(2) Dear Fred

is a difference in tenor, as is

(3) Please don't do that Nigel.

as opposed to

(4) Stop it you little bugger!

The differences among *homosexual*, *gay* and *poofter* are differences in tenor, and these reflect larger-scale differences of attitude to life and society, and in that sense are also ideological.

Tenor is also expressed in and through the function words. As an example of this, we shall look at the ways in which Margaret Thatcher

54

uses *you* and words like *have to* in the following passage. What follows refers to Text F in the appendix. *You* is one of those function words which are likely to occur in many texts, especially spoken ones. Very often the speaker has no option but to use *you* if they are talking to someone directly. But in this passage *you* is used not primarily in addressing the interviewer. When we ask ourselves what other words might have been used, we may be surprised by how many there are. Does Margaret Thatcher use *you* to stand for an impersonal *one*? Or as a modest form of *I/me*? Or does it refer to *he/she* thought of as an exemplary prime minister? Or is it an impersonal *it* as in *it is necessary that*? Or does it mean the British people, and/or government – *we*? or *they*? Amazingly, it seems that 'you' can be seen, at different points in the passage, as a 'synonym' for every other pronoun.

Let us look at some specific examples, such as:

(5) So you've got to be strong to your own people.

This follows a mention of *government* then referred to as *it*. *You* could be 'a good government' or it could refer to the leader of the government. So it might mean 'it' or 'I'. But it could also be the impersonal 'one', what ought to be done by whoever is in power. This sort of ambiguity seems to hold for the following examples too:

(6) and other countries have got to know that you stand by your word

(7) and yes, you *have* got to be strong on law and order

But the meaning of *you* is different in (8) and (9):

(8) Then you turn to internal security, and yes . . .

(9) you *can't* have law and order observed unless it's . . .

In (8) this seems to be an 'editorial' sort of *you*, indicating what 'I' want to talk about next; and in (9) it seems to be an impersonal *you*, as if the meaning were 'Law and order can't be observed unless . . .'

The overall tenor of the passage is strongly affected by the use of *you*. *You* is less assertive than *I*, and less formal than *one*, and less remote than *he/she* referring to an abstract good prime minister or *they/it* for an abstract good government.

You conveys a friendly tenor, and draws the audience and interviewer into a familiar kind of solidarity by blurring the distinction between 'I' the speaker and 'you' the interviewer/audience. It also has the effect of making the prime minister sound down to earth and less assertive. She does not say

(10) I have to be strong . . .

but

(11) You have to be strong . . .

Not

> (12) I have to create the framework for a good education
> system

but

> (13) you have to create the framework for a good edu-
> cation system

Tenor, here, is being handled very astutely to project just the right image to the radio audience: definiteness of views, but indefiniteness as to who actually controls, or who 'has got to' control things. The indefiniteness, also, might be construed as modesty, directing attention away from the speaker herself and onto the issues as she sees them, presenting her views as impersonal common sense – what 'you *have* to' do.

A similar strategy can be seen in the use of words such as *have to, got to, must can, can't, should.* Grammatically these words are all similar and, like *be*, they are very common verbs which can occur in any context. They have two main roles: they can indicate obligation or compulsion, as in:

> (14) You have to stop now.

or they can indicate 'necessity', as in:

> (15) It has to collapse under so much weight.

Margaret Thatcher uses both meanings. When she says

> (16) It has to be strong

she means that this is an objective necessity. She is describing an iron law. When she says

> (17) you have to create the framework

she is talking about compulsion, what someone ought to do, the obligation of a good prime minister. Sometimes she manages to mix the two up.

> (18) you've got to be strong to your own people

This expresses both what a good prime minister ought to do, and what objectively, according to her, cannot be avoided.

The repetition of *you* and *have to* words gives the passage its stylistic texture. It is overwhelmingly about what ought and must be done while putting the particular holder of these views into the background. Assertiveness and opinion are presented as common-sense necessity and need.

A less ambiguous example of overall textual tenor produced by function words can be found in Jeffries' (Text E) reiteration of *I* and the short sentences which are all strongly assertive without being in any way argued. It is all *is* and no *because*. Parra-Wa-Same's (Text G) tenor is one of complaint. It is achieved also by frequent repetition of *I*, as an example of a person who has lived a traditional kind of life.

The tenor of the audio-tape version of the *Pinocchio* story differs from that of the Ladybird story book primarily in its mention of *I* together with casual conversational expressions with *you* in them:

> (19) Have you ever wondered if wishes really do come true? Well, they do! And I, Jiminy Cricket, have seen it happen! Here, let me tell you about it.

You is used too to draw in the reader, as if Jiminy were telling the story in the same room. The question also draws in the reader, as does 'Here, let me tell you about it'.

✎ EXERCISES

10.1

1 Note the number of times, in Text F, the following are used

   (a) *you*;
   (b) *I*;
   (c) *should be, has to, have to, has got to*, and similar expressions;
   (d) *can* and *can't*.

2 Look at the analysis done in 1.

   (a) How many sentences do *not* have a *you* in them? Which are they? What significance is there in their position in the sequence of the whole text?
   (b) What patterning is there in the use of *can* and the words listed in (c) above?
   (c) How does Margaret Thatcher manage to make the sentences in which she uses *I* sound relatively unselfassertive?

10.2 Rewrite the following passage without using either *you* or a *have to* word. You may find it useful to say *the government* in place of *government* and a *be* word for words such as *have to, must, should, will, got to, can*. So you might begin 'The government is strong and does ...' What is the main difference in tenor now?

Quotation 10.1

I believe that government should be very strong to do those things which only government can do. It has to be strong to have defence, because the kind of Britain I see would always defend its freedom, and always be a reliable ally. So you've got to be strong to your own people and other countries have got to know that you stand by your word.

10.3 Rewrite the following passage using *one* in place of *you*. What difference in tenor does this produce?

Quotation 10.2

Then you turn to internal security, and yes, you *have* got to be strong on law and order, and do the things that only governments can do, but there, it's part government and part people, because you *can't* have law and order observed unless it's in partnership with people.

———————————————

STYLE AND IDEOLOGY

11

In this unit we look at some of the ways in which, consciously or unconsciously, a writer's or a speaker's general view of life, their values, attitudes, emotions and prejudices permeate a text.

We have seen that the style of a text is affected by what the speaker or writer is trying to do in writing or speaking (the genre), by who is being addressed and in what tone (tenor) and by the medium. Now we look at the effect of ideology, the wider conception of life and values which seems 'natural' to the speaker or writer. Sometimes this relation is clear enough, as when a woman calls herself *Ms*, when the head of a meeting is called *the chair*, or when someone says *terrorist* rather than *freedom fighter* referring to the same person. Even if thought of as dictionary entries, these particular terms tend to suggest not only a context, but wider ideological positions in relation to it. They have, as it were, an ideological 'charge'. Other words like this are *exploitation* and *law and order*, which seem to belong with left and right positions respectively if cited on their own.

Exploitation is associated with ruling-class control of the people in what is taken to be an unjust way. *Law and order* is associated with the same power relations seen now as in need of protection or strengthening. *Exploitation* takes on a challenging aggrieved ring, while *law and order* acquires an air of righteous upholding of decent people's values.

There are other ideologically 'charged' words which are common in both left and right texts, but which mean different things in each. One of these is *freedom*. When Margaret Thatcher says

(1) the kind of Britain I see would always defend its freedom

59

she is thinking of freedom in a particular way, but this is not explicit. We have an idea what she means because we have heard and read other texts by her, and by people speaking from a similar ideological position.

Ideology is also, often, a matter of grammar, that is of the role of the function words which occur in all texts, the aspects of style we looked at in Unit 6. These kinds of words are, in fact, often implied by words like *freedom*. *Freedom* implies a 'from' and a 'to', a 'for' and an 'of', which are often not made explicit. In other words, if we put things in the form of a question, the word *freedom* implies

(2) of what, from what, for whom, to do what?

If these 'of/from/for/to' slots are filled in, the ideological position becomes much plainer. This is in part due to the fact that these function words all direct attention (a) to context and (b) to who does what to whom. Rhetoricians often achieve their ringing effects by suppressing these relations. Each of us then can fill in the slots in our own way and end up 'agreeing', or at least finding it difficult to disagree.

We all agree Britain should have 'freedom', but we do not agree about the 'of/from/for/to' factor. Margaret Thatcher does return to the theme of freedom without making this explicit when, towards the end of the passage, she talks about 'people' and creativity. We can assume she is talking about freedom *of* individual competitive opportunity, and freedom *from* the 'restrictions' of socialist kinds of legislation, or trades union practices.

The freedom is *for* 'Britain', and later, 'people' and it is *to* 'rise to whatever level their own abilities can take them'.

Of course words like *opportunity*, *restrictions* and so on also need to have their implicit grammatical relations spelt out. As we look more carefully into a text we begin to see more and more of these unclear or unstated relationships, and so to appreciate how much has to be taken 'on trust', as it were, for the text to sound coherent and persuasive.

And then there are covert metaphors connected with grammatical relations. For example there is something – several things – odd, from a literal point of view, in saying that Britain would defend its freedom. Britain is a geographical entity. It cannot defend anything. So *Britain* means 'the people'. But then we must ask how 'freedom' is something you defend. Is it not rather the geographical entity, Britain, that is actually to be defended (rather then the entity that defends)? And being able to defend the country is what constitutes having 'freedom'. But then, as we have seen, 'freedom' means different things to different 'people'.

Margaret Thatcher allows *Britain* to stand in the grammatical relation of 'subject' (actor) in relation to the verb (action) *defend*, and *freedom* to stand as the 'object' (goal) of that defending. As a sentence it sounds coherent enough, but as we have seen, the surface form hides a number of unresolved debates, and to opponents may sound deliberately evasive.

In seeing the ideological patterning of the extract as a whole we need to take these points about 'freedom' and 'Britain' with the uses of *you*, and the *have to* words, which we studied in Unit 10. A point to make then is how, although the extract is explicitly devoted to 'freedom', from the point of view of the verbal patterning, verbs expressing coercion (the *have to* words) and 'necessity' (*can, cannot*) predominate.

It must not be thought that conservative politicians are necessarily any more or less ambiguous and contradictory than others. Margaret Thatcher's particularly forthright approach to politics makes her case more straightforward to analyse than some others'. Indeed ideology is often most clearly indicated by what the speaker or writer takes as obvious and assumes at the outset, and this may mean that it is often not mentioned explicitly at all. And it is this silence that controls the whole drift of a text.

Let us look at the boxing commentary. Here the ideological underpinnings are detectable only in the positive values given to aggressiveness and causing pain, and in the enthusiasm for violent competition for fame and money. So the commentator concentrates on the details of the fight, and the background he introduces lies within the boxing context: trainers, promotions and past contests, and, of course, crowd and media audience.

This seems an utterly normal kind of selection to the boxing enthusiast, but the person who is repelled by boxing will be the more struck by it. That person, of course, is not catered for at all in the commentary with its 'in' vocabulary of right-over-the-tops, holdings and ramrod left jabs. The knowledge of and attention to detail are themselves indices of commitment to boxing as a valued ritual.

It would be possible to describe the boxing context from a contrary ideological position, a feminist one, perhaps, selecting for mention the sadistic faces of members of the crowd, the appearance of the cut eyes, and frenzied screams of encouragement from housewives and bejewelled film actresses. But such an account would no longer be a conventional boxing commentary. Ideology is built into the genre.

✐ EXERCISES

11.1 In what ways could the following be understood as ideological?

(a) a beautiful girl;
(b) a handsome woman;
(c) END RESTRICTIVE PRACTICES;
(d) a superb left hook.

11.2 Politicians often use the word *people* in what we have called a 'charged' way. What ideological differences do you see in Mrs Thatcher's phrase *Over to people*, and the slogan, *Power to the people?*

11.3 The passage from Richard Jeffries (Text E in the appendix) makes an explicit challenge to traditional assumptions about time. But he also makes covert assumptions which most people would accept about the relation between nature and machines. How, if at all, does this get into his wording?

11.4 Collodi's original version of the *Pinocchio* story (translated in Text D(i)), like the Walt Disney adaptations (quoted in Texts D(ii) and D(iii)), both treat the relation between the carpenter and his puppet as being like that between father and son.

    (a) What are the unstated implications of this comparison?
    (b) What is the difference in the way Collodi treats the relation between Geppetto and Pinocchio, and the way the Disney adaptations do?

11.5 The personal ad, Text H in the appendix, is extremely indirect in what it says. But behind the indirection is a good deal of cultural history. In what ways is this indirectness itself, and the examples used, related to traditional ideologies of sex and power?

A NOTE ON THE POETIC 12

In this unit we look at verbal mime in poetry as a typically 'literary' feature of style, bearing in mind that it occurs in other kinds of text as well and is not exclusive to poetry or indeed to literature.

The study of style has, until quite recently, been associated mainly with literary style. But it has become recognised that literary texts use the same resources of language as other texts, and all those features which in the past have been associated with 'literariness' can be found in other kinds of text as well.

There are, nevertheless, features of style which are found more often, and more densely, in artistic texts than in others, and particularly in poetry and poetry-like texts such as songs, raps and some advertisements, and some comics.

One of these features is mime, that is making the sound, and sometimes the shape of the lettering, or the placing on the page, of words contribute to their meaning. The commonest example of this is onomatopoeia. What we may call 'pure' mime, of this kind, occurs quite often in comics. Here the words have no other meaning than their mimicry. Some examples are

(1) craaaaaaaaark
(2) grrrrr
(3) brmmmmm
(4) cockadoodledoo

Sometimes the words may have an ordinary kind of meaning too; but still, to many listeners, the sound still mimes that. Examples are:

(5) boom

(6) zip

(7) crash

Poets often use combinations of sounds across several words to do similar things. Perhaps the most famous is Tennyson's

(8) the murmur of innumerable bees

The same kind of method was used by Keats when he wrote of wine

(9) with beaded bubble winking at the brim

which also uses a good many nasal (*m/n/ng*) and *b* sounds, but is less directly imitative of sound, even though it has been acclaimed by critics as miming the effect of effervescence. But here the connection between sound and meaning is more difficult to account for than in (8), where the *m* sounds recall the sound of humming. Nevertheless many people accept that Keats' phrase 'works', and that in some way it is a matter of the way in which the sounds are used. Of course, we can draw attention to the *b* sounds, in *beaded*, *bubble* and *brim*. Then the nasal sounds in *ink*, *ing*, and *im*, all with a short *i* sound before them. And we can contrast these 'voiced' (resonant) consonants with the two (nonresonant) unvoiced sounds *t* and *k* (where you cannot feel your vocal cords vibrate).

But we move into speculation once we try to go further, and say, perhaps, that possibly the voiced *b* and *m* sounds suggest the swelling out of the bubbles, the sharper unvoiced *t* and *k* suggest the breaking. Then we move into the exchange of subjective responses which could hardly be established in a final way.

Such speculations are not entirely empty. If you ask people which of the following words might most suitably represent a hedgehog, and which a shiny black cat

(10) ritikepiti

(11) dloowoam

you will probably find they think that (10) 'sounds' more like a hedgehog looks, and (11) more like a shiny cat.

Another aspect of verbal mime is the use of verbal rhythm to represent 'real life' movements, most famously in Alexander Pope's lines:

(12) (a) When Ajax strives some rock's vast weight to throw
(b) The line too labours and the words move slow:
(c) Not so when swift camilla scours the plain,
(d) Flies o'er the unbending corn and skims along the main

('An essay on criticism', in *Poems of Alexander Pope*, ed. J. Butt (London: Methuen, 1963), p. 155)

The lines (a) and (b) have a larger number of naturally stressed syllables in them, and so seem heavier and slower. Lines (c) and (d) have a larger proportion of unstressed syllables, so they sound lighter and move faster. Line (d) has more syllables than the others.

The situation is complicated by the metre, since this requires an 'official' measure of ten syllables to a line, alternating light, heavy, light, heavy. As in a good deal of verse, the metrical framework is played off against the natural rhythms of nonverse speech.

Here are the syllables in lines (a) and (b) which would be stressed in a normal nonmetrical reading. They are shown in capitals (including the A of 'Ajax')

> (13) (a) When Ajax STRIVES some ROCK'S VAST WEIGHT to THROW
> (b) the LINE TOO LAbours and the WORDS MOVE SLOW

These are the lines which mime slowness and heaviness. Each contains six stressed syllables, and four unstressed.

Now look at the pattern for lines (c) and (d), where the verse mimes lightness and speed.

> (14) (c) not SO when SWIFT caMILla SCOURS the PLAIN
> (d) FLIES o'er the unBENDing CORN and SKIMS along the MAIN

There are five stressed syllables in (c), and five unstressed – the conventional verse pattern. But in (d) there are five stressed syllables and seven unstressed.

The effect of speed is produced, so it seems to many critics, by the fact that in English, the unstressed syllables have to be spoken relatively faster where there are a lot of them coming between stressed syllables. A further effect is achieved by Pope's exceeding the conventional number of syllables, stressed or unstressed, in a line.

This aspect of style is connected to metaphor in being based on comparison – between verbal and other kinds of speed or movement in the Pope passage, or between verbal and other kinds of sound in the comic strip examples.

Similar to these kinds of mime is the use of repetition of sound, not directly to imitate verbal meanings but to make a memorable phrase. Examples would be:

> (15) the God slot (repetition of 'o' plus similarly produced consonants)
> (16) stranger danger (using rhyme)
> (17) loony left (alliteration)

The repetition of sounds is not representational here, but is, in a musical sort of way, cohesive. Rhyme, of course, is often used in a systematically cohesive way in verse.

Related to these kinds of mime is JUXTAPOSITION, that is the placing together of sentences or words in such a way as to leave the reader or hearer to make a connection between them, for example, in stage dialogue.

Juxtaposition

(18) A: (watching the nature film) Vicious little beggars,
those scorpions, aren't they?

PAUSE

B: Have you seen Rogers lately?

Here the coherence is provided by the thought processes connecting
the two. This kind of connection has attracted the attention of
psychoanalysts and psychoanalytically inclined critics, who are
often particularly interested in connections which are unintended,
or unconscious, and consequently very difficult to 'prove', and the
connections adduced may be coloured by subjective experience, or
ideology, or culture.

EXERCISES ✎

12.1 You are inventing a language to be used by aliens in a science
fiction film. They are invisible but speak an onomatopoeic language,
Mimitic.

    1 'Translate' all the following English words into what you
think a suitable Mimitic sound-word would be.
    2 Arrange the Mimitic words and their English equivalents in
a random way, and ask others to guess which Mimitic word
stands for each English one.
    3 Consider:

       (a) which were easiest to guess and why;
       (b) which were hardest to guess and why.

    4 Suggest ways of making those in (3b) more 'public'.

List
square
round
fast
slow
eating greedily and talking with the mouth full (one word in
    Mimitic)
sexy
boring but correct (one word in Mimitic)

12.2 If possible do this activity with others. Look at the following
two-line juxtapositions:

    (a) In what way does the second line 'follow' the first?
    (b) In what ways are the two lines like and unlike metaphors?

       (i) At the pond children are collecting frogspawn.
          The old lady is labelling jars of jam.

(ii) The chancellor's new television has arrived.
      The dustmen couldn't find its box.

12.3 Comment on the use of verbal mime in the following quotation from a poem by e.e. cummings.

Quotation 12.1

anyone lived in a pretty how town
(with up so floating many bells down)

12.4

1 Comment on the following poem translated from the Czech of Miroslav Holub (Text I).
2 Find out what the linguist Ferdinand de Saussure said about the contrastive basis of the meanings of words.
   Could you see a further 'intertextual' juxposition between this poem and Saussure's lectures?

   Very brief thoughts on the letter M

   A, b, c, d, e,
   f, g, h, i, j,
   k, l, n, o, p,
   q, r, s, t, u,
   v, w, x, y, z.

   (Miroslav Holub, *Notes of a Clay Pigeon*
   (London: Secker & Warburg, 1977), p. 25)

FURTHER READING

The great majority of books and articles on style deal with the style of literature. However, many of these provide wider insights into the way style works in other kinds of text and aspects of life, as, of course, literature itself aims to do.

The books suggested below are broadly in line with the approach taken in this one, but they provide more rigorous or more wide-ranging studies. Some are devoted primarily to linguistic analysis, some to the wider context and broader issues to do with style, and some attempt to bring these together.

If you are interested primarily in the details of how texts work at the level of wording, it might be best to start with the books by Carter, Halliday, Hasan, Leech, and Crystal and Davy.

If you want to look into the wider issues, you might look at the books by Pratt, McCabe and Rimmon-Kenan.

The attempts to bring together wider ideological concepts and detailed stylistic patterning tend to be the most difficult, but in many ways the most stimulating. The following list gives these in order of accessibility: Halliday and Hasan, Kress and Hodge, Burton, Threadgold.

Burton, D. (1980) *Dialogue and Discourse: a Sociolingusitic Approach to Modern Drama Dialogue and Naturally Occurring Conversation* (London: Routledge).
Burton relates her description of the way ordinary conversation works to the style of conversation in the dialogue of plays, and relates both to ideology. The approach aims to bring together general ideas and linguistic analysis.

Carter, R. (ed.) (1985) *Language and Literature: an Introductory Reader in Stylistics* (London: Unwin Hyman).
This book focuses on literature but on the basis that it is not fundamentally different from other kinds of writing or speaking.

The focus is on analysis of wording, and the book provides an excellent 'next step' from the present introduction.

Crystal, D. and Davy, D. (1969) *Investigating English Style* (Harlow: Longman).
A nonliterary approach. The authors concentrate on details of wording, structure and tone of voice. Some of this book is technical, but can be enjoyed by the nonspecialist. The analysis of running commentaries on cricket and the coronation of Elizabeth II can be compared with what has been said about commentary in the present book. They give a more detailed treatment than I have given here.

Halliday, M. A. K. (1971) 'Linguistic function and literary style: an inquiry into the language of William Golding's *The Inheritors*' in S. Chatman (ed.), *Literary Style: a Symposium* (New York: Oxford University Press).
A classic of literary stylistics, and a model for any kind of stylistic analysis. Halliday relates grammatical patterning to ways of thinking and viewing experience among Golding's fictional Neanderthal men. It has something in common with our discussion of the 'omission' of *he* and *is* in commentaries.

Halliday, M. A. K. (1976), *Spoken and Written Language* (Oxford: Oxford University Press).
A readable account of the differences between speech and writing, which has implications for any study of style. As always, Halliday relates his details to wider aspects of the social context.

Halliday, M. A. K. and Hasan, R. (1985) *Language, Context, and Text: Aspects of Language in a Social-Semiotic Perspective* (Oxford: Oxford University Press).
A useful book for the student of style as it gives a readable explanation of (one theory of) the relation between language and context, and how this affects wording.

Hasan, R. (1989) *Linguistics, Language and Verbal Art* (Oxford: Oxford University Press).
The book takes a similar outlook to Halliday and Hasan (1985) but focuses much more closely on verbal art, a concept which includes poetry and fiction, and also children's rhymes and the genre of the nursery rhyme. It provides both very clear and very complex examples of the verbal patterning we have been looking at, and does so in much more detail.

Haynes, J. (1989) *Introducing Stylistics* (London: Unwin Hyman).
A suitable half-way house between the present book and the more rigorous or deeper studies cited in this list for further reading.
  Mainly non-literary in approach, this book is in two parts, the first primarily analytical, and the second and more accessible part

devoted to a range of texts from conversation to recipe, television advertisement, popular song in wider social contexts.

Kress, G. and Hodge, R. (1969) *Language as Ideology* (London: Routledge).
A more detailed account of the ways in which choice of words and structures may mask what is actually going on. It relates to our discussion of tenor and ideology, though perhaps the concept of ideology is a little under theorised.

Leech, G. (1966) 'Linguistics and the figures of rhetoric', in R. Fowler (ed.), *Essays on Style and Language* (London: Routledge), pp. 135–56.
Among other things this paper gives a clear and accessible account of how metaphor works, and relates to our discussion of metaphor in Unit 4.

McCabe, C. (ed.)(1991) *The Talking Cure: Essays in Psychoanalysis and Language* (Basingstoke: Macmillan).
This approach to discourse has implications for style, in 'slips of the tongue' ways, and relating styles of ideology and culture. The focus of the essays themselves is rather on ideas about language and ideology than on details of language.

Pratt, M. L. (1977) *Towards a Speech Act Theory of Literary Discourse* (Bloomington: Indiana University Press).
Although orientated towards literature, this study gives an admirable explanation of the less easily available ideas of William Labov on the style of conversational narrative. This view of narrative is accessible and has been very influential in thinking about written narratives too.

Rimmon-Kenan, S. (1983) *Narrative Fiction* (London: Methuen).
An admirable and readable account of the ways in which the writer of fiction achieves effects. It deals with such things as selection of detail, and 'camera angle' as well as characterisation and dialogue. A valuable background for more linguistically detailed studies of narratives.

Threadgold, T. (1988) 'Stories of race and gender: an unbounded discourse', in D. Birch and M. O'Toole (eds), *Functions of Style* (London and New York: Pinter), pp. 169–204.
In places this is a demanding paper, but it is worth persevering with, representing as it does an important attempt to bring together very wide general perspectives on ideology with details of stylistic patterning.

Ure, J. N. (1971) 'Lexical density and register differentiation', in G. E. Perren and J. L. M. Trim (eds), *Applications of Linguistics:*

Selected Papers of the Second International Congress of Applied Linguistics, 1969 (Cambridge: Cambridge University Press).
A little difficult, but worth persevering with if you are interested in what we have called 'density' and 'density of meaning' as a factor in style.

APPENDIX: TEXTS USED IN THE UNITS

TEXT A(i)
Radio commentary: Boxing, Bruno versus Coetzer (first minute of first round)

(BELL)

Coetzer the first man to come out with aggressive intent. Aims to throw an overhead right. But straight away Bruno flicking out that ramrod left jab. Coetzer slightly the taller man. Stands six foot four. And against Riddick Bowe he made a very quick start. That fight three months ago. And again here he's throwing everything from the word go. And he's got Bruno backed up in the corner. Bruno back on the ropes. Just clings and holds on. And Coetzer has come out here throwing leather. His coach Alan Taweel said that he's sometimes a slow starter. He's not shown that. There a little little left from Bruno over the top. Thudded into the head of Coetzer. And that was his first scoring punch from Bruno. But Coetzer once again on the attack, with Bruno holding on behind the referee's back. But Roy Francis spotted that one. Trying to land clubbing rights into the head of Coetzer. But once again he's on to the offensive.
(166 words)

(from BBC Radio 5, October 17, 1992)

TEXT A(ii)
Radio commentary: Boxing, Bruno versus Coetzer (second minute of first round)

Leading with an orthodox left hand jab. Coetzer with that thick moustache, his trade mark over the years. A year older than Bruno. 'Bruno, Bruno', is the shout from the crowd. So far though their hero hasn't landed anything too worth while in this opening round. First jab does get through. And Coetzer incidently has got – still got – that mark underneath his er right eye. And Bruno scored with a right over the top. But Coetzer comes back with a good left which thuds into the chin of Bruno. Bruno took it well and again holds on in the corner. But Coetzer, if anybody thought he was going to start slowly here, that's not the case. Bruno scores with an overhand left hook. Coetzer so

72

far hasn't taken a reverse step. Good left from Bruno. Coetzer felt that one. And he follows up with a right cross. And Coetzer for the first time just stunned a little. And a good thudding left from Bruno into the ribcage of Coetzer. Coetzer . . .
(170 words)

(from BBC Radio 5, October 17, 1992)

TEXT A (iii)
Boxing: Bruno versus Coetzer (third minute of first round)

. . . managed and trained by Alan Toweel out of the South African boxing family. And he said that this man is here for his last chance, and he's here to fight and fight hard. And he rams in another couple of body shots into Bruno and pushes Bruno across the ring and Bruno again forced to hold on. Bruno aims a slightly tentative looking jab, which Coetzer manages to take on the gloves. Coetzer again aims to land a couple of jabs of his own. Bruno scores with his own. Fast hands from Bruno. Coetzer going for the big left and scores, scores into the chin of Bruno. Bruno rocked back against the ropes, but not in too much danger. And there can't be too much between them. Low blow from Bruno. And a low blow back from Coetzer. Referee Roy Francis warned Bruno but he didn't say anything to Coetzer. This has been a fascinating opening round, and they're coming into the closing seconds. And it's going to be interesting to hear what Harry Mullin made of this one. But it's been a fast start from the South African.
(BELL)
(189 words)

(from BBC Radio 5, October 17, 1992)

TEXT B
Television commentary: Boxing, Bruno versus Coetzer (first round)

(BELL)
Bruno and Coetzer. And just as everybody imagined Coetzer is going to come for Bruno. Bruno won't have to go looking for him. [inaudible] ear from Bruno. The South African knows this is his last chance to get anywhere near a world championship fight. Bruno has quite a lot of reach advantage, although Coetzer is actually an inch taller. Hitting and holding.
(ONE MINUTE UP)
That storming left hand from Bruno is proving a deterrent to Coetzer. He's finding it difficult to get past it. Although Bruno weighs this massive seventeen stone six he still looks quite lively on his feet.
(TWO MINUTES UP)
Coetzer being clubbed to the head. Didn't even flinch. But once again Bruno told by Roy Francis not to hold. Coetzer with a little flurry. Certainly Frank doesn't want to take too many of these. So far Bruno hasn't come across with the really big right.
(143 words)

(from *Match of the Day Special*, BBC 1, 17 October, 1993)

TEXT C
Newspaper
report:
Boxing, Bruno
versus
Coetzer,
(material
about first
round)

Bruno . . . scaled a heaviest ever 17st 6lbs . . . Coetzer, heavy for him at 15st 10 lbs, was a fraction the taller of the two but Bruno's muscular frame was so huge that the South African seemed dwarfed. Coetzer came out aggressively and forced Bruno back at the start of the first round, which ruffled Frank's feathers a little. Within half a minute he had been warned for holding and hitting. A right hand also reddened Coetzer's face by the left eye. Bruno had to absorb a cracking left hook, landed a thumping overhand right, but then had to give ground as Coetzer got through with his share of blows in a hard, close first round. Bruno was also warned for a low punch.

(Bob Mee in *Boxing News*, 23 October 1992)

TEXT D(i)
Narrative:
translation
from original
version of
Pinocchio

Having thought out a name for his puppet, he started his work with great determination. He made his hair, his forehead, and his eyes in a very short time.

As soon as his eyes were finished imagine his bewilderment when he saw them moving and looking at him!

When Geppetto saw those two wooden eyes looking at him, he did not like it at all, and he said angrily, 'Naughty wooden eyes, why are you staring at me?'

But no one answered.

After the eyes he made the nose; but as soon as it was finished, it began to grow. It grew, and it grew, and in a few minutes' time it was as long as if there was no end to it.

Poor Geppetto worked fast to shorten it; but the more he cut it off, the longer that insolent nose became.

After the nose, he made the mouth; but before he had finished it, it began to laugh and poke fun at him.

'Stop laughing!' said Geppetto; but he might as well have spoken to the wall.

'Stop laughing, I say!' he shouted menacingly.

The mouth stopped laughing, and stuck out its tongue.

However, Geppetto did not want to spoil the puppet, he pretended not to see it, and continued his work.

After the mouth, he made the chin, then the neck, the shoulders, the stomach, the arms, and the hands.
(169 words)

(from Carlo Collodi, *Pinocchio* (London: Puffin Classics, 1974), pp. 18–19)

TEXT D(ii)
Narrative:
Ladybird
Books version
of Pinocchio

Geppetto the wood carver lived in a little wooden house with his cat, Figaro, and a goldfish called Cleo. He made lots of marvellous toys, but he had no children to play with them.

One day he made a puppet from some pine wood, and put strings on it so that it could dance. He called the puppet Pinocchio.

When he went to bed that night, Geppetto looked out and

saw the bright Evening Star shining in the sky. 'Look!' he said to Figaro, 'It's a wishing star!'

So Geppetto made a special wish,

I wish I may, I wish I might
Have the wish I wish tonight!

His secret wish was that little Pinocchio might become a real boy!

At that moment the room where Pinocchio lay began to fill with dazzling bright light. Out of the light stepped the Blue Fairy of the Evening Star, who had heard Geppetto's secret wish. The fairy waved her wand over Pinocchio, saying,

Little puppet, made of pine,
Wake! The gift of life is thine!

(from Walt Disney's *Pinocchio* (Loughborough: Ladybird Books, 1987), pp. 4–9)

Have you ever wondered if wishes really do come true? Well, they do! And I, Jiminy Cricket, have seen it happen! Here, let me tell you about it.

One starry night my travels took me to a tiny shop owned by Geppetto the woodcarver.

I sneaked under the door and saw old Geppetto working on a puppet that looked like a little boy. Geppetto put on a last dab of paint and said, 'There, little woodenhead, you're all finished! Now, I have just the name for you – Pinocchio!'

Just before going off to sleep Geppetto looked out of his window into the starry night. 'Oh, look, Figaro! The Wishing Star! Do you know what I wish, Figaro? I wish that my little Pinocchio might become a real boy!'

Moments later the room filled with light, and there stood a beautiful Blue Fairy. She tapped Pinocchio with her magic wand.

Little puppet made of pine –
wake! the gift of life is thine.

(from Walt Disney's *Story of Pinocchio* (London: Pickwick Group) pp. 1–5)

TEXT D(iii)
Narrative: version of Pinocchio by Pickwick Group to go with audio tape

. . . I cannot understand time. It is eternity now. I am in the midst of it. It is about me in the sunshine; I am in it, as the butterfly floats in the light-laden air. Nothing has to come; it is now. Now is eternity; now is the immortal life. Here this moment, by this tumulus, on earth, now; I exist in it. The years, the centuries, the cycles are absolutely nothing; it is only a moment since this tumulus was raised; in a thousand years more it will still be only a moment. To the soul there is no past and no future; all is and will be ever, is now. For artificial purposes time is mutually agreed on, but there is really no such thing. The shadow goes on upon the dial, the index moves round upon the clock, and what is the difference? There may

TEXT E
Richard Jeffries on time

be time for the clock, the clock may make time for itself; there is none for me.

(from Richard Jeffries, *The Story of my Heart*, quoted in F.G. Happold, *Mysticism: a Study and an Anthology* (Harmondsworth: Penguin, 1963), p. 359)

TEXT F
Interview:
Margaret
thatcher

I believe that government should be very strong to do those things which only government can do. It has to be strong to have defence, because the kind of Britain I see would always defend its freedom, and always be a reliable ally. So you've got to be strong to your own people and other countries have got to know that you stand by your word. Then you turn to internal security, and yes, you *have* got to be strong on law and order, and do the things that only governments can do, but there, it's part government and part people, because you *can't* have law and order observed unless it's in partnership with people. Then you have to be strong to uphold the value of the currency and only governments can do that – by sound finance. And then you have to create the framework for a good education system and social security, and at that point you have to say 'Over to people'. People are inventive, creative, and so you expect *people* to create thriving industries, thriving services. Yes, you expect people, each and everyone, from whatever their background, to have a chance to rise to whatever level their own abilities can take them.

(Margaret Thatcher interviewed by Michael Charlton, BBC Radio 3, 17 December 1985, taken from Norman Fairclough, *Language and Power* (Harlow: Longman, 1989), p. 174)

TEXT G
Oratory:
Parra-Wa-
Same

You said that you wanted to put us upon a reservation, to build us houses and make us medicine lodges. I do not want them. I was born upon the prairie, where the wind blew free and there was nothing to break the light of the sun. I was born where there were no enclosures and where everything drew a free breath. I want to die there and not within walls. I know every stream and every wood between the Rio Grande and the Arkansas. I have hunted and lived over that country. I lived like my fathers before me, and, like them, I lived happily.

(Parra-Wa-Same (Ten Bears) of the Yakparika Comanches, from Dee Brown, *Bury my Heart at Wounded Knee* (London: Picador, 1972), p. 196)

Strict lady wishes to contact gents, who would like to visit a formally dressed governmess [*sic*] or headmistress (black stockings, academic gown etc.). Or I could be your aunt, matron, nanny etc. I correct faults using traditional discipline. Sub ladies also welcome. Unhurried. Sussex Coast. letterbox no . . .

TEXT H
Personal ad with indirect statement

Very Brief Thoughts on the Letter M

TEXT I
Poem

A,	b,	c,	d,	e,
f,	g,	h,	i,	j,
k,	l,	n,	o,	p,
q,	r,	s,	t,	u,
v,	w,	x,	y,	z

(Miroslav Holub (1977), *Notes of a Clay Pigeon*
(London: Secker & Warburg), p. 25)

SUGGESTIONS FOR PROJECTS

Here are some ideas for projects in which you can adapt and develop the ideas set out in the units. They are not set out in any particular order, except that the first few, from A to K, are orientated towards gathering further texts, while L–V are orientated towards more general issues, and are sketched in greater detail.

A More on commentaries

We have already looked at radio and television commentaries on boxing. Gather some other commentaries. Some should be of 'slower' events such as a golf tournament, some of 'faster' or equally 'fast' ones such as tennis or horse racing, and others should be non-sporting, for example commentaries on fashion shows or public ceremonial occasions.

Look at ways in which these are like the boxing commentaries in style, and ways in which they differ.

B Commentary-like texts

Other texts have features in common with commentaries in being about something immediately present to the speaker or writer. Try recording a selection of weather forecasts for the same day on different television channels and radio stations. Compare them with each other for style, and with commentaries. You could extend this by looking at texts in which a person demonstrates how to do something, as on a *Blue Peter* programme on televison, or a cooking programme. In such texts the commentator is describing what they do as they do it.

C Diaries, time-tables, journals, reports, minutes

These kinds of text are all closely tied to times and dates, but usually differ in layout, and from the point of view of emotional involvement and formality/intimacy. Gather some examples of this kind of text and see how the same or similar events or times or day are treated in each, what selections the writers take to be relevant, and what emotional involvement or detachment each shows. Try to isolate particular aspects of the language which differentiate each one.

Collect a selection of texts which tell you how to do things: the label on a fire extinguisher, fire regulations, instructions for convenience foods, for a board game, a recipe, instructions on an examination booklet, a knitting pattern, a kit for a model, a sporting manual. Take some of these and see what features of style they have in common. Then, or as an alternative project, take a selection of the same kind of text, for example, a range of different fire extinguisher labels, or recipes, and look at the variations.

D Instructions

Take any well-known text which has more than one translation and compare versions of the same original passage. Make this passage as long as you can cope with so that, when you count examples, they begin to have some statistical significance. The most readily accessible examples are, probably, translations of well-established novels or poems.

E Translations and adaptations

You might also look at adaptations of English texts, such as *The Jungle Book*, for younger children.

Look at a group of different texts, all connected with the same or similar events: for example you might take your diary, your lecture timetable, a taped passage from a lecture, your notes on the passage, a book recommended in the lecture, a casual conversation later with friends, a passage from a seminar discussion about the same topic. Try to see how these differ from the point of view of genre (type of text), and how they relate from the point of view of content.

F Groups of texts about the same events

Take any passage or short text which seems to you to embody prejudices of some kind, about gender, race or class, and relate the prejudice you detect to specifics of language. Try not to restrict yourself just to vocabulary. One way of looking at this is to work with others and each do a rewriting of the passage from a different point of view. You might also use two types of prejudice text, one which is crass and another subtle.

G Prejudice and perspective

More ambitious would be to take a literary text and retell the story from a different point of view, *Hamlet* from the point of view of Fortinbras, *Robinson Crusoe* from the point of view of Friday. The best way to take this would be to discuss the overall difference of perspective in general terms, and then home in one one particular passage, or speech, and rewrite it in detail.

Look at the contents page of a fashion or other magazine and discuss the overall style. Do you see any implicit meanings in the layout of the page, and the relationship between the titles of the articles, any advertising material, the way in which they are presented, the

H Juxtapositions

illustrations, and so on? Compare the magazine with one, or more, others.

I   News items

Transcribe one particular news story from television and radio news items and a tabloid and broadsheet newspaper. Make an analysis of differences in selection, priorities given within the story, within the paper or programme, and point of view. Begin with intuitions, then relate these to details of linguistic choices. You will need to bear in mind, also, as we did with the commentaries and reports in the units, that the medium of communication affects style.

J   Songs, raps, poems, football/demo chants, shopping lists

Record two or more examples of any three items, and make transcriptions. Look for stylistic features in common. And then discuss what makes the different types of text different.

A variation on this would be to compare popular songs from the present time to those of former eras, the Edwardian 'ballad', the music hall song or Rogers and Hammerstein kinds of musical.

Or you might compare different song lyrics from song writers from the same era: Irving Berlin and Ira Gershwin, for example.

K   Story telling and written stories

Ask someone to tell you a story about a personal experience, and record it. Transcribe it with all the *ums* and *ers* kept in. Then, working with others, each make a 'literary' version of the story, that is, change it into a short story.

Then go through the different written versions looking at different ways in which the information has been used in each. After that, take one of the stories, and compare it stylistically to the original in transcription.

A variation on this would be to compare adult to children's oral stories.

L   Radio/ television times

Collect four or five different versions of the programmes on a particular television channel for a particular day. Look at different *Radio Times*-type magazines, newspapers, and so on. Discuss stylistic variations in the layout, the prioritisation and the kinds of commentaries/evaluations given. Extract specific stylistic tendencies in each example.

M   Redraftings

Take any example you can find of a finished text, literary or non-literary, together with earlier drafts. Look at each revision and decide why the author made it. There are published examples of the revisions of some of Wilfred Owen's poems, for example, or of T. S. Eliot's *The Waste Land*. Or, if you write yourself, you could use some of your own work.

Alternatively you could set yourself to write a 'minisaga', for example a James Bond novel in one hundred words. Keep the drafts and then reflect on what you had to change, and how economies of wording are achieved.

Take any poem, or piece of text in which language is used in a miming way, as described in Unit 12. Work out for yourself what the relation might be between the wording and the mime effect it produces in you. You might look at onomatopoeia, or rhythms, or you might prefer to look at concrete poetry, or the visual appearance of words in comics or advertisements. Consider how you would convince a more sceptical reader that your insights were other than merely subjective impressions or, alternatively, how you would persuade someone to share your perceptions.

N   Poetic mime

Obviously, if you can, it would be well worth asking someone else to do the exercise with you, and to compare notes.

It is sometimes said that the effect of some stylistic choices cannot be gauged objectively. It is subjective, and different people have different reactions to them.

O   Nuance and subjectivity

Devise an experiment by which you will test whether the responses of people to subtle differences of style are purely subjective.

You might consider one or more of the following:

1   Take a passage and alter it in some way and then ask as wide a range of readers as possible to read and/or listen to both versions and decide which is, let us say, more friendly, more convincing, and so on.
2   Take a quotation and comments about its effect made by a literary critic. Devise a questionnaire with a selection of possible responses with the critic's among them, and ask people to say which they sympathise with.
3   Compile a list of close synonyms, such as *sofa/settee*, *fine/fair* (weather); ask people how they think they are different, and then see what consensus there is.
4   Do an 'association test'; that is, ask people to respond to hearing an individual word by saying the first word that comes into their heads. You might want to separate the reponses of men from women to see if they differ in any consistent way.

Rewriting a passage or a short whole text in different words is a way of understanding its textual 'grain', without having to go into abstract analysis, a way of understanding style by devising contrasts and (sometimes way-out) alternative verbal compositions. You should, however, try to talk through the results you achieve, and compare with the original *after* you have done the rewriting. Here are some approaches. Do all these with one or more other people so that you can compare your results.

P   Changing the wording

1   *Rewriting*
    Take any short text or passage of about half a page (or compose one yourself) and

    (a) rewrite it without using *any* of the words of the original, with the exception of function words such as *is*, *he*, *the*, and so on.;

(b) rewrite selected aspects of it, for example
  (i)   all the nouns,
  (ii) all the pronouns,
  (iii) delete all the adjectives,
  (iv) change the verbs so they are either all formal or all ultra-casual,

(c) rewrite it in a tenth of the original length;

(d) rewrite in
  (i)   a quarter of the number of sentences,
  (ii) four times the number of sentences,
  (iii) giving half the sentences no verb.

2 *Reviewing*
Discuss your results and formulate some general ideas about the effect of different kinds of rewriting on the meaning(s) carried by a text.

3 *Testing ideas*
Repeat the same kind of rewriting as you have just done but now rewrite a different kind of text, and see if the general ideas you have formulated apply to the new text as well.

Q Flouting conventional spellings

1 Gather a large collection of unconventional spellings such as *nite*, *luv*, *Beatle*.
2 Distinguish these from mistakes both from the point of view of what the speller is aiming at and the kinds of respelling involved.
3 Can you find any broad categories into which respellings fall, or rules which respellers follow? Think of the letter structures of the words themselves but also of the tenor they produce.
4 Conclude with one of the following:

(a) a closer study of one kind of respelling, applying the work done in Unit 3 on following and flouting conventions, and relating this to the historical evolution of the English spelling system;

(b) some practical research devised by you in order to test whether respellings, and perhaps which kinds of respellings, do in fact have the effect they are designed to have;

(c) the wider significance of respelling. Interview people who are upset by spellings such as *nite*, and on the other side discuss the thesis that since business people can spell as they like, why (i) have rules for schoolchildren; (ii) have the particular rules we tend to have for schoolchildren?

Almost every comment that has been made in the units can be fitted into the wider 'orchestration' of stylistic patterning that was discussed in Unit 6, and illustrated in the analysis of Text E.

R Orchestration

Take any other text from the texts already discussed and collected in the appendix, and make a full-scale study of every possible kind of patterning you can find in it.

Go through the units to find ideas for the kinds of patterning to look for. You should decide yourself on what you want to discuss. Here are some ideas:

1 *Types of pattern*
be words,
pronouns,
length of sentences,
phrases beginning with a preposition such as *in* or *at*,
'emotive' words,
attitudinal verbs such as *should, must, can,*
sentences beginning or ending with similar words,
nonstandard usage such as lack of *be* words or verbs, or repetition of similar ideas through different words, such as *time, eternity, now,*
particular kinds of connecting words such as *and, therefore, although.*

2 *Comparisons*
Sometimes patterning (such as length of sentences, or types of sentence-connecting words) is best brought out by showing how some other text differs in this particular respect, or is the same. So it is a good idea to look from time to time at contrasts and similarities outside the text under study.

3 *Coherence*
You may find, when you come to tie up the ways in which the different patterns reinforce each other and all pull together to contribute to the overall 'grain', 'effect' and coherence of your particular text, that you want to move into interpretation. So you will have to bear in mind how far what you are saying is 'objective' or how far you find yourself 'making a case' for this or that view of the text.

4 *Presentation*
You need to spend some time early on in your study deciding how you are going to show your results, for example whether by a series of tables or by different felt-tip coloured markings on the texts, and so on.

1 Take two (or more) texts which are very similar to each other in content, and focus on the ways in which their stylistic treatment of this content differs. This can be done along lines illustrated in the units, with the different commentaries on the same boxing rounds or in the different translations of

S A contrastive study

the same story. However, you could also do a study of texts which have very similar purposes, such as advertisements for similar products, blurbs for similar videos or books, or cards which have the more general similarity of 'greeting' or 'thanking', etc.

2   Begin by focusing on aspects of the wording which can be regarded as similar and aspects which can be contrasted. Where you can, count up examples of this or that stylistic feature, such as the average number of words per sentence.

3   When you have noted a number of differences try to find some motivation for them, for example in the topic, the speaker/writer's intention or attitude, the genre, the medium of expression, or in ideological assumptions.

T Comparisons across texts

1   Take one aspect of style which has interested you, such as the use of, lack of use of, or type of use of

> *be* words,
> pronouns,
> linking words such as *although*, *when*,
> linking words such as *and*, *but*,
> locative phrases,
> synonyms/near synonyms,
> repeated sentence structures,
> metaphors,
> words such as *can*, *ought*, *should*,
> lexical density,
> or whatever you like.

2   Look at this feature in as many different texts as you can, choosing them for their differences of genre or content.

3   From your findings attempt a provisional hypothesis to be tested by further studies. The hypothesis might be of the form 'Texts using short sentences tend to be . . .', 'Texts using the simple present tense tend to be . . .'

U Selection and description

1   Work with two or more other people. Choose a 'scene-setting' passage from a novel which you judge to be relatively little known. Each partner independently rewrites the passage in such a way as to mention a completely different set of significant details, but get as near as you can to what you understand to be the artistic (or other) purpose of the original selection.

2   Compare your selections with those working with you, and discuss any patterns you find in types of detail mentioned, both in their work, and in that of the original passage. You all then make revisions where you think they are required.

3   Show the passages, including the original in typescript, to someone who has not been involved in the work and get an opinion as to one of the following:

(a) which is the original;

(b) various aspects of style you need to decide yourself: for example, which is most 'modern', most intimate, etc.

4   What conclusions do you draw from the comments you get in 3?

INDEX

Types of text (genres) are put in **bold** type. Individual words discussed in the units and/or presented in the exercises are in *italics* under 'words discussed'.